PLANETARY INTERVENTION

FABIO SANTOS
TED HEIDK

PLANETARY INTERVENTION

1ˢᵗ Edition

São Paulo

Fabio Borges dos Santos

2019

Copyright © 2019 by Fabio Borges dos Santos.

International Cataloging Data in Publication – CIP

Santos, Fabio Borges dos.

Planetary Intervention. / Fabio Santos – 1st ed. – São Paulo, Brazil: Author's edition, 2019.

Bibliografy.
ISBN 978-1-086361-25-4

1. Extraterrestrial contact. 2. War veterans – briefings. 3. War-history. 4. Heidk, Ted. 5. Military history. 6. Special forces. I. Heidk, Ted II. Title.

19-26211 CDU-001.942

ISBN 978-1-086361-25-4

Cataloging elaborated by
Maria Paula C. Riyuzo – CRB-8/7639

Edited and translated by
Fernanda Lopes

Front cover and publishing
Richard Veiga

PLANETARY INTERVENTION
1st edition: may 2019

My thanks to all the people who contributed to this unique moment in my life and to my growth as a person.

I am the result of the trust and strength of each one of you, especially my devoted wife and children and my friends who gave me strength: Dr. Maria Auxiliadora Vaz, Dr. Luiz Felipe, José Luís Miranda, Jonathan Sardenberg, Daniel Viana Contar, Rodrigo Romo, Laura Eisenhower, Dr. Rafael Lara and Dr. Tatiana Lara.

Finally, a special tribute to my deceased parents.

Ted Heidk

"I occasionally think how quickly our differences worldwide would vanish if we were facing an alien threat from outside this world. And yet, I ask you, is not an alien force already among us?"

Ronald Reagan, *President of the United States of America, United Nations General Assembly, September 21st, 1987*

INDEX

Preface 9
Introduction 13
1. SOLDIER UNDER CONSTRUCTION 19
2. RECRUITING AND TRAINING 25
3. THE FIRST MISSION 34
4. THE FOLLOW UP MISSIONS 39
5. BLACK HAWK DOWN 49
6. UNEXPECTED ENCOUNTER IN COLOMBIA 56
7. COMBAT AND CAPTURE IN ZIMBABWE 63
8. SUPER SOLDIERS AND WORLD MILITARY ACTION 71
   Secret missions 73

    The elite of the elite. 75
    Super soldiers 77

9. **ONE MISSION AFTER ANOTHER** 80
    Day off 82
    Stray bullet. 82
    Repentance in Bosnia. 84
    Sky lights 85
    Horrors of war 86
    The real reason for the presence in Iraq. 86

10. **ANTARCTICA** 89
    McMurdo 92
    The guardians of the ice 93
    The encounter 95

11. **THE LAST MISSION** 97
    Prisoner. 101

12. **BACK HOME** 103

13. **TECHNOLOGIES FOR THE MINORITY** 106
    Conscious x Subconscious 107
    Secret Space Program 109
    Corey Goode 111
    David Icke and Emery Smith 113
    Human technology 113

14. **OUTBURST OF A SOLDIER** 117

15. **SOME THOUGHTS AND INFORMATION** 134
    Antarctica 135
    Aliens 138
    Extraction of artifacts 142
    Who's in charge? 144

16. **THE FINAL JUDGMENT** 146

PREFACE

by Laura Eisenhower

In 2006, something very interesting happened to me. At a social event, I casually met someone who offered me the opportunity to – literally – leave the planet. I was recruited to go to Mars.

Many people don't believe me. You may not believe me either. I get emails all the time saying I'm crazy and stuff like that, but that doesn't bother me. It strengthens me in many ways, because truth doesn't need belief, it's just what it is.

People could actually see in the news, at that time, messages like "the Dutch foundation 'Mars' is looking for pioneers to colonize the red planet. You only need to be at least 18 years old to apply. " This was being shown on CNN.

At first, when I heard the term "going to Mars" or a "colony of Mars", I thought it was something for the future. Just a great idea that would become more popular over time. The news said that "The company 'Mars' will establish a human settlement on the planet in 2023" and asked people "what would it take for you to leave Earth forever?".

I really didn't understand the reasons or why I was involved or even being recruited. So, I thought and concluded that it was something I could easily answer "no" and continue with my happy life. I ended up moving to North Carolina in the United States to live with this person, taking my children with me. As I became more involved in this lifestyle with this person, this Mars recruitment's subject kept coming back and became even more urgent and extreme, in the sense of how important it was to go on that mission.

I got emails talking about the target date of 2012, emails that mentioned technologies like "Looking Glass" or things called "Orion's cube". These were subjects that were just going through my mind like I was in a movie or something that could also be described in this book.

But as the planned date was 2012, I recognized that this was something well planned at the time and getting away from it would not be easy as I thought.

I discovered, after six months of relationship, that my partner was specifically sent to lure me into this recruitment, while all this time I just thought I had found a person who was involved in a plan to go to Mars and I had the option of going or not.

When I found out that I had been specifically summoned to go and that if I refused, I could be kidnapped or taken anyway, I knew I was dealing with something very dangerous and I was not sure if I would go or not. It didn't sound positive, because I initially thought "well, this does not seem a terrible thing if the goal is to protect the human genome" – that was the main reason they gave me.

I just know that I have a mission on Earth. I discovered that this recruitment on Mars was a manipulation designed to program the people involved and make them believe that they're helping the human race. I saw that many very well-meaning people were stuck on an agenda that's not serving us as humanity.

It seems to me that's exactly what's being described in this book, which, in a way, applies to Ted. The choices we make may not be clear at the time we make them and can affect our lives forever.

… And there's still the extraterrestrial presence on Earth to comment on.

Valiant Thor, a non-human from Venus, reportedly met with my great-grandfather, President Eisenhower (34th US president, 1953-61), and Nixon in the early 1960s. He presented his mission, whose purpose was to help humanity. His mission, for example, was to start turning off the darkest aspects of government. He claimed to have a strong affinity for Eisenhower and Nixon.

So, president Eisenhower put him in a VIP status for three years at the Pentagon to try to help him change this whole game. The bill was rejected, and the government decided that it would not accept the help of these beings from Venus.

This is just one of the many stories of extraterrestrial beings on Earth. Believe me: they're not all positive, as you will see in this book.

What we're going to read in this book is a courageous act of spreading information. It is a detailed testimony of how occult forces act on Earth through extremely questionable interventions (or would it be manipulations?); visits to underground bases; and multiple encounters with extraterrestrial entities, some even characterize as armed conflicts. All within our own planet.

Enjoy reading it. This is one more step toward truth. It is an effort to regain control of our planet and our lives, freeing us from the control of the forces of darkness and reconnecting us to our true galactic origin.

Laura Eisenhower

INTRODUCTION

First of all, I would like to make it very clear that any information in this book referring to the performance of troops in the above-mentioned wars, whether on the secret squad or on any army in the world, is intended to expose the truth in the perspective of the people who control our planet.

We do not intend to defame the image of the thousands of men and women of the armies of different countries around the world; quite the contrary: we exalt, congratulate and acknowledge the superhuman effort and courage of those who take the oath to defend the flag of their country, whatever it may be.

This book is also dedicated to our military who unknowingly are being manipulated, that fall into the trap of patriotism and end up fighting bravely in a meaningless war, while the powerful harvest the fruits and manipulate them as they want, playing with the irreplaceable lives of these brave human beings.

With that said, let's get some thoughts about this book.

I really admire Ted's courage to come out with this information. From the first conversation I had with him on the phone, I realized that it was a person with a good heart and a strong story that needed to be told. For that reason, I immediately left my other projects aside and focused on the execution of this book so that it would be finalized as soon as possible.

But it's undeniable that such a story would not be easy to tell. Even more so because the content of some passages meets directly popular beliefs such as the existence of extraterrestrials – or, even worse, their presence on Earth – in addition to other factors such as the manipulation of wars and the command that a supposed hidden government maintains.

Here in this book we will call Ted "Daniel" to keep a certain distance from his empirical person and also so that I feel a little freer to tell the story – which's not at all a fairytale – even with some adaptations for your improvement on "digesting" all of it.

It's impossible to live up to all the knowledge Ted has. There are many stories, lots of information. So, any book of any length I wrote would not be enough to deal with the story with the fidelity and depth it deserves. So, I tried to select the most impressive passages to be counted as lightly as possible, for easy reading, but without losing the essence and importance of the information presented.

But there's still much to be told.

It's amazing to talk to someone who has lived exactly what I have studied all my life through books. He was there, he saw everything, he lived it on his own skin. It was and still is your life. I say this with great certainty because besides me, some friends whom I asked for help investigated various information about Ted and about what he reports. All of them have been confirmed by various sources. Even during his reports, Ted gave details of places – including descriptions of reliefs and things that would be impossible for someone who was not actually there and lived all that.

Everything he said coincided with our research.

But the most impressive thing for me was to know the history of the human being behind this combatant. Ted had to "die and be born again" when he left this secret Special Force. He was forced to restart his life with nothing. I'm not just talking about money and possessions. I'm talking about all the "friends" he lost, every family member who left… But worst of all is: all the history, achievements and studies that have been erased forever from history.

Imagine a person with no money, no possessions, no history of studies or diplomas, with few friends and only a couple of relatives to support him, having to start over from scratch. Literally from scratch. It is amazing to see how a person who possesses an extraordinary knowledge of international politics, strategy, among other things, can be doing manual labor nowadays – without wanting to detract from any profession. It's just a matter of being overqualified for the job.

Ted wages a new battle today. He struggles to live in this "Matrix" world in which we live in, having all that knowledge of reality that most of the world's population doesn't even suspect. He struggles with his loss of memory; with the constant threats he receives so that he doesn't tell the truth; struggles to support a house with wife and five children in the suburbs of Brasilia.

Between living with his day-to-day reality and relationships with the high rankings of the three national and international powers, Ted lives a double life: he is a Brazilian worker who bends over backwards to secure his livelihood, and he is also a specialist in politics and strategy sought by the greatest generals and politicians in the world for advice and personal favors.

In this book and in the story of "Daniel," you will see how this "hidden command" recruits, trains, arms and executes missions all over the globe. You will see how there are several secret bases, above and below the earth, with technology far ahead of what we know. You will see how it's possible that there are several secret bases, above and below the earth; how it's possible that humans have already interacted with different races of aliens for years and who are the allies and who are the enemies. No science fiction here. Real life only.

More than that, you will feel a bit of the horror that goes on wars and what the life of our protagonist became because he was part of this Special Force. You'll see how his name disappears from the map, his studies disappear and his history is erased, forcing Ted to start again from scratch without reference or support from his family or "friends". In addition to the various threats made to him when he sometimes tried to speak something that he supposedly "should not" say.

Planetary intervention is not a book of spirituality, nor of Ufology or military literature. Even if you read it as entertainment, know that it is not a documentary book, but a story based on the life of a Brazilian

warrior, who gave his life to a cause and today pays the double. From a family man who decided to tell a little of what he knows so that our conscience opens up to the truth that they want to be hidden.

I hope you like it. Enjoy the reading and open your eyes, because we don't have more time to lose.

Fabio SantoS

This book is based on a true story.

CHAPTER 1

SOLDIER UNDER CONSTRUCTION

Daniel Ling was born with 49 cm and 2,980 g, naturally birthed on a rainy Sunday afternoon in the mid-1970s. His parents had a farm near Gloria de Dourados, a city in the state of Mato Grosso do Sul, Brazil. He came into the world through the hands of a neighbor, a midwife, who was called in a rush when his mother suddenly went into labor that morning.

Daniel is the fourth son of the Ling couple and has six brothers, five men and only one woman. At that time, his mother, Vanessa, was a housewife and his father, Yun, was a farm worker. By means of their small property, they obtained food from the land and sold what was left in the nearest town to pay for general expenses in the house, like water and light, for example.

Thereby, Yun lived his first years of life, until one day he received an invitation from relatives of Vanessa and, in 1974, moved to Brasília, capital of the country. Daniel was four years old at the time.

His father was a Chinese's descendant and he never got to know about that part of his heritage. What he could gather was that his grandfather was an officer of the Chinese army and came to Brazil fleeing the Chinese War with Japan, after allegedly abandoning his military service. He arrived and settled down in Aquidauana, city of the Federal District, where he, his son Yun and Yun's brothers were "adopted" by a family of Germans.

This German family was very rich, and their farm was enormous. So much so that you could lose sight of it. Even so, everything was very well taken care of and they had a highly reinforced security. When his father was fourteen, he fled from the German farm and never contacted his brothers again. Yun always told Daniel that everyone there was constantly abused and humiliated by the Germans and he vanished in his earliest opportunity.

Daniel, who was four years old at the time, settle down in a neighborhood called Taguatinga Sul, paying rent in one of his relatives' house. Around 1978, when he was eight years old, he moved to Ceilândia city, where he spent the rest of his childhood and puberty.

He had a pleasant childhood, even though it was a very humble one, he went to public schools with his five brothers. But it was his father's story that always intrigued him. Yun was not much of a talker, but when he did open, he would comment on how much he missed his brothers. While his father stared at a blank space, he could see the sadness in his eyes – and even a few tears, his eyes glowing from his sorrow.

His mother, Vanessa, who was also from a humble background, was born in Lavinia, in the state of São Paulo, but Daniel never knew how she met his father. It's speculated that they met on some farm from the Federal District, but the issue was never a conversation topic in the family.

Daniel and his brothers liked to pretend they were at the war as kids. It was certainly their favorite amusement. From the time he was a child until his enlistment in the army, when he was a young man turning eighteen, he always played like that when possible and the games only became more creative as time passed by.

As a child, Daniel enjoyed using burnt matches and clay to build trenches on street gutters and playing war with his brothers. As time passed and innocence was gone too, they began to build weapons with PVC pipes, rubber bands and stones that they could shoot from up to six meters. They used bicycles lined with cardboard boxes like armored tanks, in a street battle in front of their house. Each day the games became more complex and the strategies of action more interesting.

Another fun game using bicycle and cardboard boxes was creating a flying saucer. Daniel and his brothers simulated an Earth invasion that would have to be fought, even by jumping off the bike in motion sometimes to "attack the Earthlings." As he reached the age of compulsory military enlistment in Brazil, in the year he was eighteen, Daniel was already listening to stories from his cousins and neighbors who were already serving at the city's headquarters. They were about the difficulty of the "quarantine", where no newcomer could leave his tent for the first forty days. In addition, it was common to hear stories about ghosts and other pranks that happened among themselves. Despite that, Daniel always wanted to serve and never cared for the stories he heard.

Finally, in 1988, with eighteen he enlisted in the nearest headquarters and asked to volunteer in the battalion. He wanted to get in. It was not long before the good news arrived, he would be accepted in the 32nd Brazilian Army Battalion – and he would stay there for a year, until 1989, which was not only celebrated by him, but also by his family, especially his father Yun who perceived his son following his grandfather's footsteps in some way.

On his early days, he took a liking on shooting. Every time he put his hand on a rifle, he remembered his child's play with his pipe, rubber band and stones, feeling the gun as part of his body. He looked like he'd been shooting for years!

Luckily, when he joined, the quarantine was no longer required and with only a week of service, you could return home. At that time, they also changed the output uniform, which would be a pair of green pants, military boots, an ogri shirt and a beret. That was how he got home for the first time where he was greeted with a kiss on the cheek by his mother and a smile from his father.

Daniel spent a year serving as a soldier. As he applied himself, had sharp results and had an "unfriendly" face, as it has always been a part of his personality, he was standing out among the group. From the beginning, he noticed that two lieutenants were talking more to a group of people than to the others that were there. Slowly, they began to approach him.

At the time, he was eighteen and an army newcomer, so Daniel wanted to keep pushing the good impression and fulfill his dream of pursuing a military career. In one of the conversations with the lieutenants, Daniel then remembered a story that his father told him as a child, where his uncle was a member of the FARC – Revolutionary Forces of Colombia. A very famous terrorist group in Latin America, with great strength in the country next door. Yun told him about a payline that happened inside Brazil, probably to let drugs and weapons come in and out freely from both countries.

Daniel then told the Lieutenants everything. He revealed the details about what his father told him, including names, modus operandi, weapons used, mules schemes (people who are paid to cross the border with contraband), places, including drawings on a map. He imagined that this would win the confidence of the lieutenants, which would help him with his career. Besides contributing with the security of his country, of course. As he told his story, he began to wonder if it really was an uncle or if it was not his father himself, so much so that the story was rich in detail. Besides, his father mentioned that he no longer had contact with his brothers ... How could he know that, then? He put all thoughts aside.

From this day on, he began to be treated differently not only by commanders, but also by his colleagues. His reserved personality and hard work during training made his teammates bet each other to try and see who could get Daniel arrested over the weekend for bad behavior or some flaw. Several jokes and attempts were made, unsuccessfully. There was a lot of jealousy in the air, because besides being on the spotlight, he was also the best of all in shooting, strategy, night compass, etc. In internal team competitions, he was always the leader of his group and invariably his performance led to victory.

Daniel even became part of an enlistment propaganda that the army did on national television in 1989. At the time, he was shown in uniform, guns in hand, and serving as an example for the youth. A voice in the background said "Enlist now."

His first year of service was coming to an end. Daniel searched for the official means to pursue a career, since it had always been his dream since he was a boy. He decided to take the cable course (the next patent after soldier) in which he was approved, but he was not able to find vacancies. At that point, he came across reality: only relatives and close friends of high officials got the jobs, regardless of their performances. Being the best from the barracks that year was not enough for him to get a stop and pursue his dream job.

After all the effort he made during that year, being the best in all the areas trained from the whole quarrel, he realized there was no chances to stay in the next period. It was then that, with his worked-up head, he addressed the lieutenant and asked to be part of the first discharge (layoff) at the end of the year. The lieutenant tried to persuade him to reconsider his decision and maybe try something next year-but it was only in vain. Daniel was hurt and determined to end his path through the Brazilian army.

When he got home that day, his father wasn't there. When Yun arrived hours later, he told his son about the conversation he had with the colonel and that his discharge would be given. Daniel still doesn't know the reasons, much less the content of his father's exchange with the colonel. But one thing was certain: he was no longer part of the battalion.

CHAPTER **2**

RECRUITING AND TRAINING

Then came the day when the farewell ceremony of the soldiers who dropped out in 1989 happened. Daniel, despite being reserved and even envied by his colleagues, was a good person, and he insisted on being there. The event was a tradition for the battalion, and everyone participated. On that occasion, he was greeted by everyone, from fellow soldiers to the colonel – the one who had talked to his father days before – and was praised by everyone. "You're going to be missed," that is what he heard the most.

A sergeant even recommended that he got into ESA – Sergeant's School. At that moment, very disappointed by all that had happened, he thanked the nomination, but refused it. His head was already made up and he still felt bitter. Now, he would focus on his life apart of the army, even though he didn't know very well what to do yet.

At the end of the ceremony, Daniel left the barracks and turned right towards the battalion's corner. About forty meters ahead of him was the bus stop where he would have to wait for his transport. In the middle of his path, he remembered that he forgot his backpack in the locker room and had to go back. Upon arriving in the courtyard, there were still some people there, so he was greeting and waving to all his acquaintances again on his route.

On his way back, with his backpack in hand, he crossed the whole army yard again and reached the barracks' door. The sun was intense, the heat was high, and the only shady place between the barracks and the bus stop was in the army parking lot. From there, he could see when the bus arrived and could rush towards it, while taking advantage from the shadow that one of the entrance's columns projected where he was.

While paying attention to the name of the bus, someone touched his shoulder from behind. When he turned around, a well-dressed, dark-haired man, about his height, asked

without blinking: "Would you like to pursue a career in the army?" He readily said yes, but not that year because he had just left his terminating ceremony. The mysterious man then said that he had seen it and if Daniel really wanted to pursue a military career, he would call him, so that the mysterious man would "find a way." He left a piece of paper with a phone number in his hands, entered a golden-colored Opala, which stop by him in that same moment and was gone. At that moment Daniel saw his bus already at the stop and ran towards it, he got in the vehicle in the very last minute, almost having to leave on foot.

As he entered the bus, he placed the paper with the mysterious man's phone number in a pocket of his backpack. Three months passed by before Daniel could remember this piece of paper again. During this time, he tried everything: he talked to relatives, friends and neighbors about all kinds of work possible. He tried to help relatives on their duties, he did some job interviews, but there was no way. His passion for the army spokes louder.

It was then that Daniel decided to call the number from his backpack to see what would happen. He felt there was nothing left to lose. On his first attempt, the person who picked up the phone asked him to call again the next day at the same time. That's what he did. On his second attempt, the person on the other side asked where he lived and if he really wanted to pursue a military career. He answered the two questions and heard the following message: "Perfect! Now stop talking and focus on your results. Tomorrow we meet at 3:00 pm next to your house. "

Still not knowing what to expect, at the next day Daniel was in front of the store next to his house at the settled time. It was then that the same four doors golden Opal stopped before him and inside were the same mysterious man driving and two more people in the backseat. He then entered the passenger seat and the car took off.

Now the mysterious man had a name: Mark. Probably not his real name, but the apprehension of not even knowing the names of people was over. Marcos was very receptive, friendly and kind throughout the entire journey. They talked about different subjects like politics, music and little things. Nothing about where they would go or what they would do.

It was then that they arrived at Brasília's Air Base, next to the airport. A military installation. At the entrance, the gates opened immediately, and Marcos didn't even stop the car. He drove to one of the tracks and stopped the car at the base of one of the parked aircrafts. At that moment he turned to Daniel and said, "Whatever you do from now on, do not open your mouth. Your dream will now be fulfilled". Daniel would never see Mark again. He got out of the car and was amazed by plane. It was the first time he'd ever fly in his life. He couldn't tell which model it was, but he saw that it was gray and medium-sized. He climbed about ten steps on the front latter of the aircraft and as he entered, he noticed that there were not too many seats. There were about ten people inside the plane and there some seats left. Each one sat in a corner, for it seemed that nobody knew each other. The others, like him, had no luggage. Daniel traveled only with his body clothes and without knowing his destiny.

The afternoon was ending when the plane finally took off. One of the people who seemed to be in charge offered drinks and food to everyone. Daniel refused because he had eaten before leaving home and didn't feel hungry. A short time later the aircraft landed near the city of Três Corações, in the state of Minas Gerais, Brazil. Some cars were already waiting for them on the track and they were all taken to a facility next to the Sergeant's School (ESA) in the area. Curiously, this was the exact spot that years later, in 1996, it was destined for the famous "ET of Varginha" – the ESA from Três Cortes was the place revealed as the first stop of the aliens' bodies supposedly captured on that occasion, according to studies from the ufologist Marcos Petit, also revealed in one of the episodes of the Brazilian series "Ride with the UFOs", shown in 2018 on the History Channel.

It was not exactly inside the ESA where Daniel was taken, but it would be a spot next door where some huts were set up. It was there that everyone settled down and Daniel had six more companions in one of the tents. They provided clothes, food and everything they needed. So far, no information had been given on why they were there.

The next two days were entirely devoted to medical and physical evaluations and general guidance on the location and what was being done. It was said again on the occasion that everyone should keep as a secret everything they saw and heard, and not leave the perimeters of the lot, and that they were to receive the best military elite training in the world.

In the next fifteen days the training was intense. They had physical exercises in the morning and a medical follow-up in the afternoon. They were treated as an elite troop, reinforcing the importance of secrecy and the expectation that in the coming days all training would be in the form of a selective eliminatory process. There would be no fault tolerance, no matter how small. Daniel was happy and felt at home. He could not be more motivated by all that, and the air of mystery only added to his conviction.

At the end of that period, when they woke up in the morning, they all marched about five miles into the woods to the top of a nearby mountain. There were three helicopters, being two used for transport and one as a medical unit. They all entered the aircraft and flew for about an hour and a half. They reached a well-isolated and unidentifiable area, where they were again in cabin huts for another month at the same pace of training and routine as before. Until then, something quite similar to what Daniel had experienced in his year of service in the Brazilian army. But the mood was different. His companions seemed to be on a level above.

A month passed by quickly and they were again displaced. Now they were in a military area in the state of Rio de Janeiro, again in campaign camps, where they spent three days in a training focused on weapons like M-16, FAL 762 and 9 mm pistols. At the end of seventy-two hours, they boarded on an airplane bound to the Amazon. There, the seven recruits spent about ninety days in combat and survival training in the jungle. This training is so ferocious that out of every ten foreign military personnel who do it on Brazilian soil during exchanges with the Brazilian army, only three complete it. Of the seven recruits who arrived in the Amazon that year, only Daniel and two other companions would complete the training.

Thus, the three approved went by plane to the 5th Naval District on the beach of Casino in the state of Rio Grande do Sul, where they spent some days doing parachute training, soon after embarking again to the border of Argentine with Chilean Patagonia, in the southern part of the American continent, to spend the next sixty days in amphibious training, the so-called COMANF – maneuvers on land and on water, including professional military diving. The routine intensified and Daniel was amazed at all that.

All three were approved so far and they went to the Tangara da Serra's military base, in the state of Mato Grosso, for training in high temperatures. Summer was close and the exercises were done with equipment that weighed about twenty-seven kilos, and often the recruits were completely covered. Daniel saw his body reach all its limits in the forty-five days that he passed there, experiencing temperatures of over forty degrees Celsius every day. At that time, in addition to the three recruits, there were eight members of the support team, including trainers, doctors and rescuers.

Again, upon conclusion of the course, they all flew to a remote city between the states of Goiás and Tocantins. But this time they returned to the classroom for theorical instruction in combat. They talked intensely in the next twenty days about details in armaments, like disarming bombs and fighting strategies. In the end, a written test was made with all three and again they were approved.

By the end of 1991, as the theoretical training was approaching its end, an officer entered the classroom and said that there was an emergency call, and everyone would be called in and they would have an hour to get ready. Without knowing where they would go, as always, they flew to Cuiabá military airbase in the state of Mato Grosso, where they picked up another Hercules aircraft bound for Gibraltar, at the European point closest to the African continent.

Arriving at Gibraltar, the three recruits landed and stood in line waiting for their command for hours, when they were finally separated to never meet again. Daniel took a flight to a nearby country where he waited for instructions for three days and then was taken to a base of the Foreign Legion in France.

Arriving there as the only Brazilian, he had contact with more recruits from other countries like United States, England, France, Spain, etc. He could observe people from all over the world through flags in their uniforms. He was put on a training team with one more American and one British. Daniel did not speak the language, but gradually learned with the help and goodwill of his companions. In the beginning, he communicated by gestures and then he learned the first words until he could communicate reasonably. He stayed there for about ten days when they were called to board again.

Daniel and the two companions then wore NATO – North Atlantic Organization uniforms – and flown to Bosnia. They were told it was a combat mission and more details would be given upon arrival.

The landing was made on top of a mountain, on a very short track. It seemed that the pilot and the plane were accustomed to the difficulty of the place. At the landing, Daniel spotted four tents – the same as his training in Brazil. The next three days would be instructions on the local conflict between Serbs, Bosnians and Croats and what they should do if it was necessary to use force on any of them. It was not clear "on which side" they were. Clearly, they were within an area of intense conflict, with no good guys or bad guys.

The medical check-ups were daily on all thirty-six men who made up that elite battalion at that time, where Daniel was the only Brazilian.

At the end of the three days of information and exams, a curious fact. Daniel saw American agents wearing uniforms from NASA (Space Agency), FBI (Federal Police) and CIA (Central Intelligence) arriving. These agents would spend the next four days talking to all thirty-six men in the camp about instructions in case they spotted UFOs (unidentified flying objects), from which equipment they use up to procedures in case of fall and extraction of vehicles, part of them or even of possible occupant. Notice that at that time no information was given about aliens, even because UFOs are unidentified aircraft and not necessarily from another planet.

At the time, Daniel thought it might be from some country or countries that would be interfering with the local conflict without NATO endorsement, but in the last three hours of the briefing the agents mentioned that it was possible to meet "nonhuman" entities. Questioned, they showed the whole team photos of different types of entities, followed by some recommendations such as: not touching entities with clean hands (always wear gloves), protect areas with risk of exposure such as neck, feet, shoulders and hands, do not breathe close to the creatures – always keep one meter away, at least, among others.

After a day of rest, in the following afternoon, everyone was called in the briefing hut and the following message was given: "You will have a mission for tonight. Let's go up the mountain located northwest of the camp. We have a suspicion of genocide. ". At that time, a local military guide was introduced to talk about the land and the details of the road. With all the agents, medical and military at that moment, the group added fifty-five people.

Like this began the first official mission of Daniel in this elite troop.

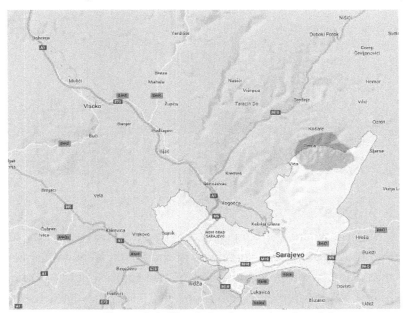

FIGURE 1: The capital of Bosnia Sarajevo and, northwest, the city of Visoko, approximate location of the troop.

CHAPTER **3**

THE FIRST MISSION

The base where the command was located was in a valley near the town of Visoko, northwest of the Bosnian capital Sarajevo. In that place, a space with the size of two football fields (200 m × 100 m) was prepared and from there the helicopter flights took off to the combat zones.

The whole team was ready. They left the final briefing place and walked all the way to the waiting helicopters with their engines running. They took a flight to an area near Lake Modrac, next to the city of Tuzla, in the northeast of the country.

Arriving at the site for the final instructions, they were given the necessary equipment for the mission. It was the first time Daniel had seen that kind of technology. What caught his attention the most was a helmet that had a digital camera with motion sensor and another digital camera on his rifle. The two were linked to a type of external HD implanted in the helmet to collect the information in real time.

Nowadays this information can be very common and simple, but not at the time, since the year was 1993. There were no digital cameras commercialized for common population, although the technology was already presented in the 1970s.

Some officers stood by the helicopters in this new camp, and thirty-six men, including Daniel, set out for the next mountain. Upon entering the woods, the commander sent a radio message to the main camp requesting a reinforcement in the rear. Minutes later, more than 100 NATO's guardian men arrived on a joint mission with the UN, who had been instructed to stay about thirty meters behind the elite command. And so they did.

The commander of the elite troop then instructed his men to remain calm in any situation, to avoid giving unnecessary shots, and to be alert at all times, that includes helping their comrades in case of any difficulty in regard to the instructions given. At that moment they put on their masks, began to communicate only by signs and then set off in formation up the mountain.

Arriving almost at top, they observed something that Daniel will never forget in his life. A non-human creature of short stature (about a little over a meter tall), who collected human bodies from what may have been a confrontation between Serbs and rebels. There were bodies everywhere. This being stacked them in a kind of "box" that housed two bodies at the top and two bodies at the bottom – it looked like some kind of preparation for transport, like a ship's container.

The elite unit watched the work of this being for about four minutes. It was then that the creature realized that it was being seen. At that moment, Daniel took a photo with his rifle that pointed to the entity (original image below).

FIGURE 2: Being photographed by Daniel's rifle.

In the image above it's possible to see the creature with a rifle in hand, which was taken from one of the bodies that it carried. On the stones around it, you can still see the rest of the blood being drained from the bodies before being withdrawn.

The commander, in the instructions at the foot of the hill, had made it very clear: the mission was to capture, alive or dead. It was then that the chaos began. Shoots all over. Two more creatures appeared from behind the stones. The three beings moved with a speed that caught everyone off guard. Despite their size, they were very stiff and strong and began to strike the nearest soldiers with astonishing force and violence.

As the three beings found themselves trapped at the top of the mountain, their only exit was by the way the troop went up. One of the beings passed Daniel's side at a great speed and bumped into his rifle. At that moment, with the immense violence of the stride, he fell to the floor almost unconscious. When he had regained consciousness a few minutes later, the three aliens had disappeared, and a strange silence had taken place. The general report? Between the elite troops at the front and NATO tactical support at the rear, seventy-three were killed in the confrontation and 15 were missing. From Daniel's unit, there were five deaths. One of them, the American who had done training in his closest group a few days before.

Daniel didn't quite understand what had happened. In fact, nobody understood. How could three beings of that size have such speed and strength to kill more than seventy men ready for combat? It was impressive to see the bodies only with external bruises, without any perforation. The impact of a bullet was so strong that could rupture internal organs. No weapon, no shot was given by "nonhuman" creatures, none of which were captured..

They took the wounded back to the camp. Daniel had only a few bruises on his left side due to the fall, but nothing to worry about. All the survivors stayed three days in observation in the camping due to the physical contact with those beings. In that time, several questionings and interrogations about the mission were executed by those same agents of NASA, CIA and FBI that gave the briefing of the mission hours before in the camp. Daniel had not noticed before, but this time he paid attention. The agents had a not very common appearance. They were all tall, blond and somewhat yellowish eyes. White skin, almost pale, and a voice with a very serious tone that certainly could be heard from a great distance without the need of electronic equipment.

After three days, all returned by helicopter to the camp near Visoko to continue with the training and await further instructions.

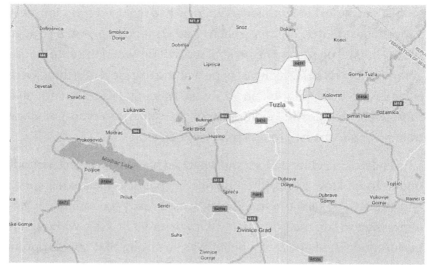
FIGURE 3: The city of Tuzla, Bosnia, and Lake Modrac, in the region of the reported combat.

CHAPTER 4

THE FOLLOW UP MISSIONS

For a long time, Daniel and his elite battalion comrades acted in various regional conflicts in wars that happened at that time, usually supporting UN and NATO troops. The missions were mostly focused on objectives that would not be well accepted by the general public, but largely implemented in such situations.

A good example was his next mission shortly after returning to camp from his debut in combat and the strange conflict with nonhuman beings. It was focused on eliminating combat cells from Serb rebels. Mission of execution, shooting to kill. The unit invaded the place informed and shot all its members. Daniel was a soldier and did what he was told by the command, without a question. Exactly how it works in a military command, especially in situations of war and conflict.

It's important to understand what was happening in Bosnia at that time, through the text below taken from the Wikipedia page.

> *The Bosnian War was an armed conflict that occurred between April 1992 and December 1995 in the region of*

Bosnia and Herzegovina. The war was caused by a complex combination of political and religious factors: nationalist fervor, political, social and security crises that followed the end of the Cold War and the fall of communism in the former Yugoslavia. It involved the three ethnic and religious groups of the region: the Serbian Orthodox Christians, the Roman Catholic Croats and the Bosnian Muslims. It is the longest and most violent conflict in Europe since the end of World War II, lasting 1,606 days. The war lasted just over three years and caused around 200,000 civilian-military casualties and 1.8 million displaced people.

His last fifteen days in Serbia were very intense. He had practically one mission a day and almost always went through unusual situations. His training, from the very first day of recruitment, besides involving physical skills of shooting, resistance and resilience, also encompassed the psychological part of the troop. They were trained to "dehumanize" themselves, that is, to suppress their feelings around any situation and focus only on the mission. Not exclusively because of the emotional impact of an encounter with nonhuman beings, but also because of all the consequences of what they witness in a war. Compassion could lead to strategic error or hesitation, which could lead to death.

In one of the missions during these last days in the country, Daniel and his troupe were arriving in formation to a small town. From a distance, they spotted a special military binocular that some rebels had conquered the village and could see also several bodies scattered all over the streets. Some of them were still in celebration, giving celebratory shoots and hugging each other. As they approached, they had a real sense of what was happening. There were exactly forty-three heavily armed rebel soldiers, who had wiped out all the men and children there. Only the women were left, who were coldly raped by some, and then killed by their rapists with a bullet in the head.

Daniel and his troops observed what had happened and asked the commander what action they would take. The commander checked via radio with the central unit, which promptly responded that the decision was non-interference, since what happened had no relation to the mission of the troop and the consequences of the possible interference would not contribute in any way to its objectives, besides the risk of unnecessary casualties. It would be a distraction.

Daniel, though angry inside and wishing to shoot the head of one of the criminals, had to obey the order and retreat back to the nearest camp with his companions. Everyone there was trained not to feel compassion, because situations like these were a commonplace and they could not divert attention and focus on the mission they were given. They were treated like robots by the command, being interested only in executing what was commanded to them. Nothing more than that.

At the end of this period in Bosnia, the entire elite unit was transferred to southern Iraq, almost on Kuwait's border, west of the town of Zubayr. At the edge of the desert there was a camp in the same way as the previous one, with tents that would serve as a dormitory, hospital, dining room and interrogation and briefing rooms.

Iraq at the time was just out of the so-called Gulf War. The explanatory text below came from Wikipedia and serves as a reference of the situation at the time.

> *The Gulf War (August 2, 1990 until February 28, 1991) was a military conflict between Iraq and US-led and United Nations-sponsored International Coalition forces with the*

> approval of its Security, through Resolution 678, authorizing the use of military force to achieve the release of Kuwait, occupied and annexed by the Iraqi military under Saddam Hussein.

According to the BBC Brazil site, *in June 1993, US President Bill Clinton authorized air strikes against Iraqi intelligence service headquarters in response to the attempted assassination of the former President George Bush in Kuwait two months earlier.*

The site Correio da Manhã from Portugal reports the attack:

> *The attempt to assassinate George Bush Sr. consisted of blowing up a car loaded with explosives when the former US president arrived in Kuwait in 1993 on what would be his first visit to the emirate after the 1991 Gulf War. According to the Northern Secret Service, if this plan failed, it was expected that another car would be bombed near the place where George Bush was to receive an honorary degree, and there was a third alternative that consisted of a suicide bombing. After several people had been detained in Kuwait in connection with this case, and following the investigations, the CIA and the FBI concluded that the explosives that the terrorists were preparing to use had been provided by Iraq and that the Baghdad secret services were involved.*

The missions of the elite command were basically to undermine the Iraqi resistance informally linked to the government of then-President Saddam Hussein. This resistance was essentially made up of ex-military personnel, well-seasoned personnel from the time of the war against Iran (1980-1988), in cells containing three to twelve people. The reason for this small number of unit fighters was to make it difficult to track their actions and the flexibility to perform surgical missions, stepping in and out of sight.

Daniel and his comrades also worked at that time on Iraqi territory, training clans against the government and therefore in favor of the UN and its NATO allies.

After several militia cell elimination missions, with and without partnership with the anti-government clans (the Taliban at that time was one of them), the elite command headed into the desert region for a survival training with NATO, which would last about a year. The climate and geography of the area were nothing like what American and European soldiers were accustomed to. Already aiming for operations in the near future, NATO asked the elite command that its troops be trained and the request was executed. Daniel then became one of the training instructors.

During this year in the desert, Daniel was summoned for missions on three occasions and all with one goal. Look for an artifact called Vimana. It is a kind of flying saucer as described in Hindu literature. The meaning of this word varies, but basically it means "temple" or "palace of a god". In the drawing below, one sees a vertical section of a Vimana described in the Hindu Ramayana book.

RUKMA VIMANA

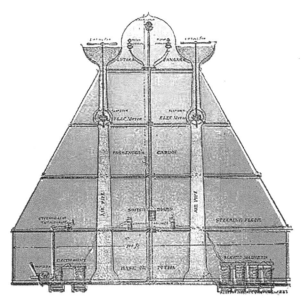

FIGURE 4: Drawing of Vimana according Hindu's tradition. Credit: Internet.

In the three missions that Daniel participated in Iraqi territory, two of them found the Vimanas. The probable locations were given by the intelligence sector that located them via satellite and the troops went there to ensure that the artifact was actually in place, as well as leaving it ready for extraction and transportation, also making sure the whole procedure was secure. Usually, they would be buried in ruins or mountains and the team would leave everything ready for a team of scientists to come and remove it.

Another team managed to find the third Vimana that the elite team Daniel was part of didn't find. He learned a few days later during training, as a colleague commented. It appears that in this case the extraction was extremely difficult and the Vimana was damaged, but no further details were given.

Completing the Iraqi's desert survival training successfully, Daniel and his companions sailed to Syria, where they would spend a week "settling," as the commander said. Nothing new, just routine training.

After that week, they spent a few months in Lebanon also taking part in missions to eliminate resistance and surgical interventions in local conflicts. Basically the same modus operandi of missions in Iraq.

In one of these missions, as the troop was approaching a Lebanese village along a trail amidst rocky mountains and forests, several rebels were sighted blocking the path. Immediately, the troop entered combat formation and minutes later the shooting began.

The combat took place when Daniel's troop was climbing one of the local hills, so in the middle of the shooting they went into the closest forest to camouflage. The rebels were up there and they were firing down the hill. Then Daniel, who was shooting wildly to see if the rebels were backing off a bit, went into the "right shot" mode – where the soldier starts firing to kill one by one.

As Daniel was firing, he backed up a little and hid behind the trees to protect himself between shots. It was like this, shooting slowly, but killing one by one, patiently. In one of these moments, he slipped, tripped over a branch that was on the ground near the tree and fell. At that moment, he rolled down the hill and felt a kind of "gelatin" suddenly envelop his body. It was strange. As he rolled, he saw the sky at times and at other times the ground. In one of these moments looking at the sky, he noticed something strange. It was as if a disk-shaped cloud with the "milky" color was just above it. He realized that he had not heard the shots before. Daniel was slowly stopping until he lied flat on his stomach.

At that moment Daniel thought he was dead. "So that's how it's to die," he thought. He was still lying on his stomach in the "gelatine," and he realized that he was in a high grass, unlike the ground where they were before, where dry land surrounded the trees on the mountain. In his head was a movie: his whole life, his family, everything that happened until that moment. This only reinforced the idea that he had died.

At last he got up and most of the "gelatin" flowed to the floor around him. To his surprise, there was no one around him. He was not in the same spot of combat. Daniel was not sure yet whether he was alive or dead.

After a few seconds, a military vehicle with four alleged officers arrived at the scene. They were a doctor and three soldiers in uniform. Daniel, frightened, aimed his weapon at them, for he did not know whether they were impostors, a confrontation with enemy soldiers or not.

One of the soldiers in the car asked Daniel to calm down. He then warned that he would not lower the gun and asks for the password, as he would shoot. This password was a phrase that special operations soldiers knew to recognize if they were in a rescue situation or something. The leader of the car answered the password correctly and Daniel lowered his "gelatinous" rifle.

The car was composed of four seats in the front of the vehicle (a driver and three passengers) and a transport module in the back, like an ambulance. Daniel was taken to the back where two other doctors were. Two soldiers remained in the front and two others were with Daniel and the other two doctors in the back, because he was informed that tests would need to be done immediately.

Daniel then asked where he was, asked about his companions, and told briefly what had happened. The response of one of the doctors was that he had been transported to that place and that there had been some genetic changes in his body, so the urgency of the tests. In addition, they explained that he was found by the intercutaneous placement implant that all special soldiers have on his bodies. Daniel was found more than 250 km from the site of the battle. They gave no further details.

As the vehicle went its way, no matter where it was going, the soldiers collected their clothes and their weapons and stored them in insulated labeled containers. Daniel then wore a plain navy blue jumpsuit and began his physical examinations right there. When he tried to pull more conversation with the soldiers, he was alerted by one of them through an eye movement that there were some cameras in the vehicle watching everything that happened and that he should be silent. That's what he did.

Daniel then began to notice what he felt about the way the vehicle was going. A few moments later he realized that he was traveling on asphalt, but in others he had the clarity of being on dirt roads or stones, because the trepidation was greater. After a few hours in this situation, he began to notice that from time to time he felt a "chill down his spine," as if the vehicle were descending some steep road at a reasonable speed to cause such a sensation.

After a few minutes the vehicle stopped. The back doors were opened and they went down. Daniel was in a sort of big garage, with no windows or any opening that could get any clarity in. He was taken to the pedestrian door at the back of the compound and realized that it was certainly a military base there, because security was strong and all were in uniform and heavily armed. All the doors were double and the second door opened only when the first one closed. Cameras were all over. Soldiers armed in every corner. To move from one enclosure to another, only a few authorized people would go ahead and use their fingerprints and also the iris of their eyes, when it was probably safer rooms, even more restricted confidential access.

Daniel would then spend about three days inside this underground base doing physical examinations, without further news of what happened, where he was or his companions and going through endless interrogations. In one of these questioning moments, he remembered the moment when he saw that disc-shaped "cloud" with a "milky" appearance as he rolled down the hill wrapped in "gelatin". At that hour he had the clarity of vision: it was certainly a ship. The detailed image of the vehicle came to his head and he managed to remember from the bottom of the ship with its details of colors, lights and size. For some reason, he decided not to tell everything that happened to the officers. The feeling was not of complete confidence and he felt that something was not right.

After seventy-two hours Daniel was taken back to his troop camp by the same vehicle and had the same feelings from when he was coming, only with the feeling of being "up" this time through gravitational pressure. About 45 minutes later, he was at camp with the other special forces recruits.

It was then that, on their arrival, as if they were waiting for him, they were transferred to Somalia.

CHAPTER 5

BLACK HAWK DOWN

The movie *Black Hawk Down* was directed by Ridley Scott and released in 2001, winning the Academy Award for Best Sound Mixing. He reports an operation based on a true story that occurred in October 1993 in Somalia during the Civil War in the so-called Battle of Mogadishu. According to the film, an American elite force was deployed to capture generals obeying Somali leader Mohammed Farah Aidid. But two UH-60 Black Hawk helicopters were knocked down and the operation, which was expected to take around half an hour, became a 15-hour battle, ending with 19 US soldiers killed and 73 wounded, and 1,000 Somalis killed, according to official statistics.

Let's understand the context, according to the text below from Wikipedia, which sums up very well the conflict portrayed in the film.

> *In January 1991, the dictator of Somalia, Siad Barre, was deposed. His departure left a blackwhole that drove the country into complete anarchy. The clans and militias who fought together to overthrow the dictator began to turn against each other for the spoils of power, initiating a new and*

bloody civil war. Between September and December 1991 at least 20,000 people were killed or wounded in fighting. The capital, Mogadishu, was the scene of intense fights between several groups and ended up in ruins. One of the most powerful Somali warlords, Mohamed Farrah Aidid, wanted absolute power and took control over most of Mogadishu and a large portion of the Somali countryside. Their militias attacked stations of humanitarian aid, confiscating supplies destined to the population. Supplies such as food and medicine were forbidden to areas controlled by groups rivaling his. The humanitarian situation in the country, which was already bad, became chaotic and it is estimated that 300,000 people died, mainly from starvation.

The United Nations responded to the political and humanitarian crisis in Somalia and sent the UNOSOM I operation. The United States launched its own operations, such as Provide Relief and the Unified Task Force (also known as Operation Restore Hope) led by the Marine Corps. Still, the death toll (in December 1992) reached almost 500,000 people, with another 1.5 million being driven out of their homes.

In March 1993, UNOSOM II was launched with the aim of re-establishing order in Somalia. But just like the previous UN mission, progress has been slow or almost imperceptible. Earlier this month, a peace initiative reached an understanding among the main groups of the civil war, but the faction of Mohammed Farrah Aidid refused to accept the results of the talks. In June, Americans began launching occasional military operations to try to capture Aidid. The following month, an American AH-1 Cobra helicopter fired at a compound where

> supporters of Aidid were supposed to be assembled. At least 60 people were killed. Four foreign journalists were killed as well. This action brought international condemnation to the UN mission and Somali civilians began to harbor mistrust and even hatred of the US military presence in the country. On August 8, 1993, possibly in retaliation, a bomb exploded during a patrol of American soldiers, killing 4 soldiers. The United States had already substantially reduced its presence in Somalia, but this attack forced President Bill Clinton to respond. He ordered that JSOC special troops, especially Delta Force men and Rangers (elite units of the United States Armed Forces), under the command of General William F. Garrison, move to Somali territory for the purpose of capturing or killing Aidid. However, after weeks of fruitless incursions, Garrison has come under increasing pressure for results.

Daniel commented that supposely about seventy percent of what is reported in the film is not true since he was there almost all the time following everything through special monitors, about twenty-five miles away north of the capital Mogadishu. He adds that one of the theories of the real reason for the military presence in the region was to cover up his elite team, because on his second day in the country he would receive a rather strange mission. The SEALS (American Marine Elite) teams and the DELTA (Special American Forces) always questioned why the elite troops Daniel belonged owned weapons, equipment, and aircraft in greater quantity and better quality than they did, without satisfactory answer. They were always trying to pull off a conversation to try to get information from the elite soldiers, obviously unsuccessful.

FIGURE 5: Crew of the Super 64, the second american helicopter shot down during the battle. From left to right: Winn Mahuron, Tommy Field, Bill Cleveland, Ray Frank, and Mike Durant. Source: Wikipedia.

The clash of the conflict was observed by Daniel and the team. Days before the famous conflict, all was well. That's when six soldiers who were out of the US battalion decided to go have fun in the city. It did not take long before they got into trouble and started a shootout at a local bar. The problem was that one of the dead on the Somali side was the son of one of the guerrilla's most powerful bosses. The suit served as a fuse, and revenge came in the famous battle four days after that.

Daniel and his companions observe on the monitor that the American troops did not find in their incursions by the city no heavy armament in the hands of the rebels. He watched soldiers firing wildly, while the rebels strategically positioned themselves on top of the buildings, executing certain shots. The response was with bullets that hit civilians, including women and children, who entered official statistics as part of the "1000 rebels killed in confrontation," as well as other details omitted by the official authorities. In addition, one of the helicopters that crashed was not knocked over, but had a mechanical problem. The consensus in Daniel's troop was that the mission had been misjudged and early authorized by the generals, since the soldiers showed a lack of knowledge of the modus operandi of the rebels and also of the geography from that region. Despite what happened, they were in place if they were called for reinforcement, which was not necessary or was not authorized.

The next day, all of the elite troops woke up early as usual and were summoned to the briefing shed. The mission would be to protect the authorities who would arrive at a place yet to be revealed. Everyone was ready in an hour, they traveled by plane to the north of the country, near the Gulf of Aden. The region was very remote, full of stones, a very dry land and there was not a living soul in miles away.

No member of the elite force knew when the authorities would arrive, much less who they were. In fact, there wasn't much sense of where they were. They then began to set up the perimeter of security, as they were trained. It consisted of four rings of security:

1st ring: it was the outermost layer of the perimeter and was about 12 km from the protected site. It was made by locating sensors that were thrown from above by military aircraft, all around the circumference of the perimeter. They were like metallic "petecas" with antennas that detected any presence and movement of any living being. Each had a range of 300 m to 1 km away.

2nd ring: several men separated by a distance of 30 meters from each other, approximately, made the patrolling within a radius of 8 to 10 km of the protected area. These are the warning soldiers. Anyone who could possibly pass through the perimeter of the external radars would certainly be approached by this team.

3rd ring: again the antennas "petecas" were placed in this perimeter. They were about 3 to 6 km of the protected area.

4th ring: the last barrier of protection was made by the troop where Daniel was. It was between 2 km and 500 m from the place to be protected. If by any chance a being passed through the first three rings, it would surely be felled without any attempt at conversation or explanation. The order was to kill first and ask afterwards.

If by chance someone could get through them, the order was to blow up the site at zero distance to protect the authorities who would certainly have been evacuated from the scene at that time. For this, bombs were placed in strategic locations.

It was almost the end of the day, and everyone was ready. Almost twenty-four hours passed, it was the end of the next day, when they were told that the authorities were coming. Daniel was in a vehicle that had a kind of crane with a basket at the end, as a fire truck and was up there as a sniper with an excellent view of the site.

About three hours later, four military vehicles black colored arrived. From within, nine officials left. All men, human, wearing dark suits. A few moments later, a high-speed ship swept across the sky and stopped above the scene. It had a very intense glow and Daniel had to take off his night vision goggles to see it in detail. His light illuminated everyone and he could see everything that was happening. The ship, which was about a hundred meters long (the measure of a football field), then began to descend and, as it came closer to the ground, their light diminished. It was oval at the bottom and flattened on top, with three "buds" on top and lights followed throughout its perimeter, from one side to another.

The ship then stopped a couple of feet off the ground and, without touching it, opened its door that was like a commercial plane. Instead of a ladder, the entrance was a ramp through which two humanoid beings emerged, floating a few centimeters above the ground and measuring about three meters high. One of the beings made a signal with his hand and four of the humans were floating inside the ship. The door closed and one of the humanoids stood outside with the remaining five delegation humans, but without interaction.

Three hours passed when a strong light appeared from the side of the door where the being stood close and the four humans appeared out of nowhere without the door opening. At the same time, the humanoid that was outside disappears and the ship begins to rise slowly increasing again its luster and causing the dust of the ground around him come up and covering the human entourage that were present. Daniel then removed his night glasses again and observed the ship leaving at an astonishing speed disappearing in the sky in a few seconds.

Without any questions, as always, everyone gathered their equipment and returned by plane to the base near the capital a few hours later when they finally had a period for rest, before continuing with the training routine and exams.

During his career, Daniel would go through about seven missions similar to this one. Usually these encounters were made late in the day, early evening, to hinder the observations from naked eyes. Putting together all the missions, there were about nine different species of nonhuman entities observed by him, where four of them caused some sort of problem for the team. In three situations there were armed clashes between the entities and the elite troops and in one of them it was only in a hostile attitude, without corporal or warlike confrontations.

CHAPTER 6

UNEXPECTED ENCOUNTER IN COLOMBIA

It was already mid-1995. Daniel and his elite force found themselves in South America, going to Argentina. They arrived at the airport of Ezeiza, in Buenos Aires, and moved quickly to an adjacent military air base.

At that moment, they immediately met with other specialized soldiers, two Uruguayans, four Argentines, two Peruvians, four Chileans, four Colombians, two Venezuelans, Daniel and one other Brazilian. The sergeant was American, accompanied by an English lieutenant, the last mentioned two being the commanders of the team, therefore totaling twenty elite men and two commanders.

They spent the night at the military base and flew the next day to Colombia. They landed at the military base of Apiay, about 120 km southeast from Bogota, where they spent the night.

The next day in the first hour, they drove by helicopter to the mountains near the Venezuelan border, around El Tuparro National Park's region in eastern Colombia. During the flight, one of the commanders briefed them on the parameters of the mission, until then mysterious. They had to find a cave that could be used by drug traffickers for shelter or weapons storage, something very common in the region, especially at that time. When found, they should mark the entrance with infrared compresses to serve as a guide for the F18 military aircraft to bomb the target and seal the entrance, making it useless.

Arming for this mission was different. Each soldier carried two 5.56 M4A1 rifles with suppressor and grenade launchers M320, ten cartons or thirty projectiles, two 9mm Glock pistols, six hand grenades, a pair of night vision goggles, a headphone-like device with a small antenna, long range lanterns, GPS location chips, high resolution microcameras, plus food in bars for two days.

The uniform was also different: it had two outer protective layers, leaving no space for any part of the body to be exposed. In addition, they completed with special gloves that had two small batteries that connected a kind of protective web inside the uniform. Despite all this, Daniel and his companions did not find the suit heavy by their standards. They then proceeded to the point of infiltration in a military helicopter model Sikosrky CH 54 and descended into a depression in the forest in the middle of a fog. They all disembarked and the helicopter was gone.

After walking for about five hours, they arrived at what appeared to be the entrance of the cave. It had a perfect circle on a rock, certainly made by laser, it looked like polished concrete, measuring approximately three meters in diameter. The entrance had a sloping angle of 32 degrees down and was all full with dead animals around it. There was no vegetation inside the tunnel, only around it, making it difficult to identify. A small cloud close to the ground was noticeable, like a fog or those dry ice effects, common in children's parties.

Then everybody was ordered to explore the cave with caution and entered military formation. When they were about 150 meters in, everyone began to feel ill at a moment's notice: nausea, difficulty breathing and a lot of coughing. It was very strange and everyone began to look at each other not knowing what was happening. The English lieutenant pulled out a strange device and pointed it towards the tunnel, and after a few seconds he asked everyone to put on their masks.

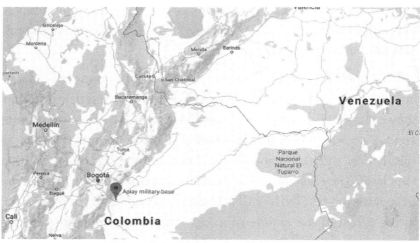

FIGURE 6: Colombia's border with Venezuela.

After putting on masks and catching their breath, they continued the mission. The cave was composed by several large rocks and a kind of grass that reached waist high, as well as small trees. As the troop came down it got warmer.

When they reached the bottom of the tunnel, about 500 meters from the entrance, they noticed that it was in a much larger tunnel that crossed the mountain from north to south. They then illuminated the phosphorescent pathway every 70 meters, ensuring that they could get back to the entrance without problems. Looking west and then south, they noticed a curve 300 meters and another about 500 meters to the east, all measured by a digital device that the lieutenant wore, so they found exits to the east. The leader gave the command and when they entered the east tunnel, an almost unbearable heat came and even the masks prevented them from breathing.

This new discovery, which would later serve as an outlet, was filled with dead animals, as well as approximately thirty bodies of Colombian army soldiers. Apparently, some were ordinary people (civilians) who also died with bullet holes, so Daniel and his companions marked that place with explosives, in addition to the infrared bombs that were already at the cave's entrance. The idea was to close the cave on the Venezuelan side, which was at the end of the tunnel that was the largest and best made.

They continued walking another hundred yards into the tunnel, when they heard sounds that seemed to be of iron hammering in iron. At this point, it was about twenty yards left to reach the end of the tunnel on the Venezuelan side, when the sergeant ordered through a signal that they stopped and stayed still without making a noise.

When Daniel looked out, he saw a metal platform – like aluminum – suspended in the air and above them were cages, like cells, inside there were people, humans. They were men, women and children who cried and sometimes yelled for help. It was an agonizing moment for everyone. Daniel was in the front of the group and took off his mask to see better. The lieutenant then asked others to do the same, but he did not like to see him without the mask. At that moment the lieutenant told everyone in perfect Spanish: "Do not move or we'll all die."

It was then that Daniel could see the soldiers who guarded the platform: they were four strong beings, but very strange with a monstrous aspects. They looked like humanoid-shaped lizards and were about 2.50 m tall, with a large head, pointed ears and orange eyes, they wore a sort of vest attached to the body, a wide belt with compartments and bracelets that looked like cell phones and carried objects similar to a rifle, only larger and anatomically shaped. Their skin was a kind of scaly or leather, resembling a lizard skin, in a greenish-brown tint.

At that moment one of them looked at the tunnel where they were and the sergeant gestured "quiet!". It was a moment of apprehension, because at any moment they could be discovered. Everyone was alert and ready to pull the trigger. Then the lieutenant pulled a device that looked like a radio transmitter. When he turned it on, everyone felt a kind of numbness in the head through their ear device. He aimed a strange, anatomical weapon that he kept under his backpack toward the monstrosity that stopped for a moment and turned back to the platform.

Later on, the sergeant told everyone that the illuminator used by the lieutenant prevented the creature from seeing all of them there and protected them from their telepathic powers. At first Daniel did not understand what he meant by that, but he did not worry too much.

Daniel watched the creatures through his binoculars, when the sergeant asked, "what are you doing?", he said: "I want to see the hostages." The sergeant then replied, "You will not like to see what's in there," but he continued. It was then that he realized that there was a second cage and the beings that were in there did not scream, they did not look like the hostages and they were not people, humans as those of the other group. His eyes were black, without the white part, and when one of them opened their mouth, he had two rows of teeth, something he had never seen.

Suddenly the beings and the platforms disappeared in a very weak kind of blue light, as if it were a cloud that formed around the cages and the monstrous guards, but with a disgusting smell. Then they put on the masks again and scanned the spot, they set up more bombs as planned and left quickly.

On the way back to the Colombian's side, Daniel noticed that the entrances and exits were ducts that led to a small center where the cages were, but he had not been able to see details because the bombs' detonation time was near. Only a few minutes after passing the first signs, the explosions were heard and everyone began to move faster towards the extraction point and waited for the helicopter that brought them back.

The military helicopter, a Sikosrky CH 54, took them all back to a base in a village where there was an airstrip and landing strip. Arriving there, a jet plane took them all back to the military air base and from there they went on a flight to Ezeiza airport in Buenos Aires, again in Argentina.

Upon arriving at the airport, they were all taken to a distant room, a small building where there was a North American officer and an NSA agent. They questioned them separately about the mission and warned them to remain silent about everything that happened. The agents kept all the equipment they had including the uniforms, but overall they were very well treated and received custom-made civilian clothing.

In sequence, all were taken separately to the boarding wing, where Daniel embarked on a flight to São Paulo, Brazil. He did not buy any tickets and did not go through normal security measures and passenger checks: he was simply put inside the plane. Arriving in São Paulo he went to Brasilia by bus. On the road, he thought about what he did and heard, and about what the agents said on their way to Buenos Aires: *"we know who you are, do not tell anyone about this or things can get very ugly. Long story short, you can end up dead!"*. Daniel never saw the other Brazilian who was on the mission.

Going back home, he thought that fiction films are not 100% fiction. There is a truth full side that nobody tries to reason with, also we are not alone on this planet, we are not the only intelligent beings and we are no on the top of the food chain. Religions are human fantasies, what they are preaching doesn't exist, just like governments, we are slaves for slaves!

CHAPTER 7

COMBAT AND CAPTURE IN ZIMBABWE

The year was 1998 and everybody was accommodated in a mobile camp south of Sanyati, about 150 km west of Harare, Zimbabwe's capital.

Although he was awake since 5 A.M., Daniel waited for the trumpet and at 06:30 he joined the others in line for breakfast. They were all quiet, eating and talking about the area and newspaper's topics.

The elite troops had been in the country for two days, and they were always wearing uniform, due to the constant possibility of missions that could eventually occur in any shift. After breakfast, they all went to physical education and weapons maintenance activities, followed by practice conferences. One part of the group went to the shooting booth and another to the meeting room, reviewing the videos produced by drones, which showed the areas that should be controlled and occupied, as well as guerrilla activities in that region.

At that moment the siren was activated so that everyone would hurry to the meeting room. In five minutes, all twenty-eight soldiers were in the room. Subsequently, the United States Lieutenant, the sub-commander, entered the room and explained the mission parameters, giving the group one hour to get ready and equipped in block formation in front of the Hercules C-130 Lockheed military transport plane, which was already positioned on the track.

It was about 09:30 P.M. when they flew for one hour and twenty minutes to the jump point, an open area in one of the depressions of Mount Nyangani in Far East. They jumped over the low clouds and landed in an area next to a watercourse with spaced out trees, low vegetation knee high, but with some prickly shrubs. The hot sun made them leave the helmets open for better ventilation.

FIGURE 7: View from Nyangani's Mount, in Zimbabwe.

After collecting and hiding the parachutes, Daniel and his companions walked almost four hours. Inside the mountain's jungle, they stopped and formed a defensive perimeter with a radius of forty meters. During that stop, the major and a lieutenant explained the parameters of the mission. It was summed up in a probable and eminent confrontation with one or more reptilian creatures, the mission was to capture them, alive or not, if the mission did not work out and to avoid deaths. In addition, they should signal the site with infrared to implode it with bombs from a military jet.

After a thirty minutes break in the defensive perimeter, they marched through the jungle, oriented and observed by the command from that moment on by satellite. Then the high-resolution cameras on their helmets and chest triggered and the uniform protection system turned on. After more than an hour in the jungle, they noticed a small group of armed men upfront. They were guerrillas, but they were frightened and made disoriented movements. They made a contact signal that was quickly flagged positively. They came to meet the troops in a surrender position. They were interrogated and revealed a confrontation they had a few hours earlier with "huge creatures of monstrous appearance" – the dread was visible in all. The survivors who were there, seeing their group die, fled because they could not stop such entities. They also said that their group had about 120 men, but many died and they did not know what happened to the others because they chose to flee.

The guerrillas were tired, scared and thirsty, though there was a small waterway nearby. They were afraid to fetch water and reported that one of the creatures left the riverbank and attacked them while the other came out of the woods, forcing them to split.

At the end of the deposition, Daniel and the others set up a safe perimeter so that three of them would fetch water, which was done, and provided cereal bars for them. They were then directed to head northwest on the trail that had already been made. The armament was given back while they received instructions about safety on their journey.

The night was coming, and with it the cold. Luckily, the uniform they wore regulated body temperature. Soon they were back on march and an hour later they were in one of the natural ridges of the mountain with low vegetation and spaced out trees with three or four meters tops and among the stones there was very low grass as in the savannah. But a little farther on, the trees narrowed and their canopies covered the spaces out.

It was then that they spotted a dead and dissected cow. It had no eyes, no tongue, no genitals, and had a cut in its belly from which all internal organs had been removed. There was no blood on the spot, which indicated that the creatures were nearby, since the cow was not rigid. A little farther on, they found an opening in the middle of two rocks with vegetation around it. They decided to enter and after five meters they found a triangular shape cut on the rocks. It was a perfect cut, creating a small tunnel about six feet long with smooth walls, similar to a marble plaque. "We must be near", thought Daniel.

They were very careful. The uniform insulation system was always on and the weapons were ready to fire. One by one, they walked in until they passed and came to a large, half-dark cave with only a few rays of sunlight, entering through a large hole above the treetops. Next, they placed the troops around a tunnel's exit, since there were also soldiers near its entrance. They spread in triangular formation, about four to six meters apart, with slow movements as they went on. It was then that they noticed movements about 100 meters ahead, on a 20 degrees slope. At that moment, they crawled through the vegetation carefully until they were at a safe distance and camouflaged.

Some creatures were sitting. One was standing and making head movements similar to a meerkat, while the other two mutilated some animals and guerrillas' bodies they had killed hours before. Daniel realized through his infrared glasses that they placed the organs inside a cylindrical container, similar to dark aluminum pots that fit together. Only one of the creatures did the job as a coroner and the others watched and gave him cover. After the organs had been removed, they placed the bodies in a box that was not sized correctly due to their distance from it, but it was noticeable that there were more vessels like these, which floated a few centimeters from the ground.

The creatures were about 2.5 meters tall – although they did not stand erect, always half-curved – they had a yellowish-colored scaly skin with parts of their back in a greenish tinge, a large head with several small tips, yellowed eyes with cat-like pupils, strong arms and legs, with long hands with four finely tuned fingers. They wore a dark vest that had compartments with objects on the sides and the right arm had a kind of bracelet in the same color as their skin. They all wore a sort of small spear, similar to a staff, and wore a kind of boot that had no shoelaces or zippers. The shoe was knee-length and had a greenish-brown color.

After a ten minutes observation, the troop began to make a triangular siege around the three creatures, keeping a safe distance. They took long because it was necessary to observe carefully, to know what they carried and to install some devices similar to small three-pronged antennas along the formation, preventing a possible reaction, so that the damages were minimal. But the unexpected happened and one of the creatures noticed their movement and came to make sure that everything was fine. That was when the confrontation began.

Daniel was in the lower part of the triangulation with eight heavily armed men at five to six meters distance from each other. The beings movements' velocity made shooting difficult. Guns were shot; it was an intense firefights and explosions for about twenty minutes. They retaliated by firing a beam of bluish light, similar to neon light, but very fast, so much so that hit several soldiers. Some who were hit hard got calcined. Those who were injured had body parts burned, practically incinerated by the shot. One of the creatures was shot in the arm that carried the weapon, but it attacked the soldiers anyway and there was a disproportionate body fight. The reptilian being punched the soldier who threw him a few yards away, leaving him with broken ribs, a broken arm and several bruises. This same creature also invested in the others and, luckily, someone hit him in the back and made him retreat, taking in that moment several shots in the region of the thorax and the legs to finally come down.

The other creatures were also injured, but were able to disappear with the containers, metal crates and bodies in a fainting bluish-colored smoke that quickly fell apart. But before it fell apart, the soldiers threw fragmentation grenades into the cloud. The interesting thing is that they did not explode or fall, they just disappeared into the air. They had to get out of there fast, and during the confrontation, five Black-Hawk H-60L military helicopters were already approaching, one of which was just to take one of the creature that had been captured.

This creature weighed something around 200 pounds, making its removal out of the cave difficult. While searching the creature, the American lieutenant prevented everyone from removing anything that was in the possession of the entity. Daniel could see and touch his garment, which seemed to be glued to his body. A hard and rough vest, which contained compartments with something inside, but could not be open. The boots seemed to have been made for his feet, the bracelet went from wrist to elbow, and his weapon was very light. Daniel noticed that the creature had three bullet holes in the back and neck, but only a small trickle of blood.

In the search with the other soldiers, they found the weapon he carried. It looked like an automobile vacuum cleaner; at one end, it was an arch that hugged the arm and a finger socket. When it was placed near the body of the reptilian, the weapon lit a very weak violet light.

Time was short and everyone was moving to leave as soon as possible, as they thought the beings could come back with reinforcements to rescue the companion who was left behind. Everyone stood in an area where the helicopter pilots could see them and, one by one, the Black Hawks got out and pulled everyone out. After a few minutes, everyone listened to explosions' blasts made by fighters jets through the flags placed earlier. It was night now, and the visualization of what was happening was already compromised.

The wounded and dead on the human side were also quickly evacuated by the H-60s that descended through the hole in the roof of the cave, since the ground did not present difficulty for this, where they took about fifteen minutes to withdrawal all.

Summary of the confrontation: two whole troops were killed instantaneously, three soldiers wounded – one with N3 (unrecoverable) gravity and the other two were in a position of relief and clash if necessary.

During evacuation, the troops who did external protection reported that as soon as the shooting ended, they saw a dark cylindrical shaped object leaving the mountain and hovering for a few moments in the air, until two glittering spheres were attached to it and in a rapid acceleration it disappeared north of their position. They were scattered around the entrance of the cave, if any of the creatures escaped in their direction.

The helicopter carrying the captured creature was accompanied by two Apache helicopters and took a different turn from the others.

Arriving at the camp just outside Harare, Zimbabwe's capital, two refrigerators trucks were waiting for them and, as they descended, were directed to get into both trucks. Inside they changed their clothes and left it inside aluminum boxes, which were numbered according to each one of the soldiers. These trucks circulated for the time needed until all were met with standard instructions' uniforms. At the moment, when descending already in Harare's basis, it was 2:00 A.M. when they entered again in a military airplane model model Hercules Lockheerd C-130 and were taken to Mozambique. During the journey, they were directed to forget the mission and not to comment it in any way with anyone under any circumstance, under penalty of martial law and probable death sentencing

Arriving at the Maputo's airbase, all were taken to medical examinations and interviews with a team of CIA / NSA agents, but at this time they were already divided into small groups.

After the release, Daniel did not see and had no further contact with the rest of the group. He was taken to an inn near the airport, where he stayed for a day and the next morning around 10:30 am, he was taken and placed on a flight to Brazil.

CHAPTER **8**

SUPER SOLDIERS AND WORLD MILITARY ACTION

Anyone can visit the US Air Force website and look in the "careers" area for the profile of the person they want to meet, as well as the open positions. It is a modern website, very well done, with lots of interesting photos and videos.

> *"The men who are part of the US Air Force Special Operations are a special breed of warriors. Their job is to push the limits by being mentally tougher, physically stronger, and ardently committed to serving our country and protecting our freedom. A job for the best of the best, this elite team of heroes goes where others will not because they are trained and ready to do what others can not."*

It looks a lot like the description of Daniel's work. I am not here to discuss the praiseworthy motivation that leads a young person to enroll in such a program and to question their bravery and abilities.

They really are awesome. The problem lies in the manipulation that these people are suffering and the possible consequence in their lives.

Let's briefly review this speech. Although Daniel has never been part of the American air force, the speech is very similar and, in the end, they all serve the same command. Expressions like "overcoming limits" describe well what we are seeing so far. We are following Daniel and his companions, and we see that these are individuals who go beyond all limits in every way. Not only in the physical, explicit in "physically strong," with trainings and situations that are beyond the physical reach of the overwhelming majority of humans on planet Earth, but also in the mental limit; not only by meeting with nonhuman beings and all that entails but also witnessing unimaginable war horrors that will surely change the mind, character and perception of all involved. These are traumas that can take forever to be overcome. Not even the most "mentally tough" soldier will escape this easily.

But it is in the phrase "committed to serving" that we have the biggest trap of manipulation. With the excuse of serving the homeland, this manipulative Hidden Government causes young soldiers to commit atrocities and become organic war robots to serve their domineering interests, whether through the creation of wars, interventions to favor one side or the other, and as we are accompanying, serve as backup for encounters with extraterrestrial beings.

In the promise to "do what others can not," this command manipulates young people using their patriotism and a little with their ego to be the best at all to serve the malevolent interests of these beings.

SECRET MISSIONS

Once inside an army or military command of any kind, their "soul" belongs to them. I say this in the sense that in this situation you should follow the given orders and period. Without questioning anything in favor of discipline and focus. After all, what would a battle front look like if every soldier questioned his superior? But this also has other consequences. One is the existence of many secret missions with suspicious goals.

According to the Military Times website, in the November 6, 2018 publication entitled "Report reveals formerly secret operations in Africa," the US military has a number of operations on the continent. Well, I do not remember having some American territory in Africa, so what are they doing there?

The official version is "Degrade Al Qaeda and ISIS affiliated terrorist networks in the Middle East and specific regions of Africa." But is it really the case? What are the US really doing in countries like Nigeria, Kenya, Libya, Somalia and Cameroon? In fact, according to the same publication, "the US military was conducting missions in at least 20 African nations. Most of them are limited to air strikes or advise, train and aid work with allied government forces". Well, we saw a bit of how this goes in this book. The truth is that young people are dying to serve the interests of the few. Official figures indicate more than 2000,000 American troops on the continent. But we can not know the real number.

The concept of current performance and the SFAB, which would be basically a brigade for training allies. But just imagine: in the 1990s the US trained Al Qaeda to fight its enemies in the Middle East and we already know what the consequences were, or at least what they claim to have been the consequences. Who are they training now? There is no guarantee that they would not be your enemies tomorrow. And the question no one wants to ask is: is it not done purposely?

Governments alternate in power and everything remains the same. As commented by the website politico.com, in a report on July 2, 2018 titled "Behind the US Secret War in Africa," actions on the continent come from the previous governments, through Obama and now Trump.

We are talking about the United States because it is the greatest military power on the planet and also the military center of the secret government (Pentagon – located in the capital Washington, DC), but the same thing happens with other governments. It is not American exclusivity. Countries on every continent are part of this military coalition that forms the task forces of this secret government, as we are also following with the story of Daniel.

The famous television network Al Jazeera posted on its website on August 8, 2011 (so we were already in the Obama administration) an article entitled "The Secret Military of the American Army." In that text they comment that "US special commands are deployed in about 75 countries around the world – and that number should grow." They were 60 countries at the end of the Bush era and estimated about 120 countries in the early Trump era. Conclusion: they are worldwide.

FIGURE 8: The Pentagon – US Military HQ and Secret World Government.

Al Jazeera adds that this "is evidence of a growing clandestine power elite in the Pentagon, waging a secret war in every corner of the world." But a war of who, for whom and why? Under the excuse of terrorism, the secret government does what it wants.

THE ELITE OF THE ELITE

The Business Insider website published on April 17, 2017 an article called "the top 8 elite special forces in the world". Below we follow the ranking in the countdown of 8 to 1:

8. The Special Services Group in Pakistan is better known in the country as the Black Storks because of the commandos' unique headgear. Training reportedly includes a 36-mile march in 12 hours and a 5-mile run in 50 minutes in full gear.

7. Spain's Unidad de Operaciones Especiales – or the Naval Special Warfare Force, as it has been known since 2009 – has long been one of Europe's most-respected special forces. Established as the volunteer Amphibious Climbing Company unit in 1952, it has since become an elite fighting force.

6. Russia's Alpha Group is one of the best-known special forces units in the world. This elite antiterrorism unit was created by the KGB in 1974 and remains in service under its modern-day counterpart, the FSB.

5. Few of the world's counterterrorism forces can compete with France's National Gendarmerie Intervention Group, or GIGN. The group is 200 strong and trained specifically to respond to hostage situations. It claims to have freed more than 600 people since it was formed in 1973. It is against the law in France to publish pictures of its members' faces.

4. Israel's Sayeret Matkal is another of the world's top elite units. Its primary purpose is intelligence gathering, and it often operates deep behind enemy lines. During the selection camp (Gibbush), would-be recruits endure hardcore training exercises while being constantly monitored by doctors and psychologists. Only the strongest get in.

3. The British Special Air Service, known as the SAS, is the infantry counterpart to the Special Boat Service. Their insignia bears the phrase "Who dares wins." Asked about the importance of the SAS's role in the fighting that followed the Iraq War, US Gen. Stanley McChrystal said: "Essential. Could not have done it without them."

2. The UK equivalent of the Navy SEALs is the Special Boat Service. The selection process involves a grueling endurance test, jungle training in the rain forests of Belize, and combat survival training, which involves intense interrogation of candidates. And you get only two attempts to pass.

1. The US Navy SEALs is arguably the top special operations force. Created in 1962, the Sea-Air-Land operators go through years of training and, especially after 9/11, endure an incredible operation tempo. Many foreign militaries base their special ops on the SEALs.

Obviously, the command that Daniel participated in is not on the list. In fact, it does not appear in any official report. As we saw earlier, their training was heavier than those described by the American SEALs – and undoubtedly, also their operations. Remembering that this is just a command. Imagine the others that must exist on and off the Earth.

SUPER SOLDIERS

There are several military theories, concepts and experiments – official and unofficial, on the subject. Let's go from the "lightest" to the scariest.

The Pentagon has already officially released its intent to get US soldiers to control combat robots with their minds. The idea may seem tempting, as we would no longer have the need for life-threatening combatants, but there is more to it than that.

The US Department of Research and Development (DARPA) has "dreamed for decades with the merging of humans and machines... such changes would have extensive ethical, social and metaphysical implications," according to The Atlantic ("The Pentagon's plans to program the soldiers' brains," published November 2018). While the excuse (given to the public to continue to have official research resources) is to improve the lives of people with physical disabilities, behind the scenes the secret government thinks of merging man and machines and making super soldiers.

This leads to a long discussion about what human beings really are and how far we should take technology. But in this military case, it seems very dangerous for me to cross that line, because I believe it is inevitable to use this technology to finally take away the emotions or any other impediment for the soldiers to carry out their missions. Better than a robot, it's a man with the ability of a machine – working in symbiosis.

In the same November of 2018 the famous Reuters agency published an article called "Pentagon looks to exoskeletons to build 'super-soldiers,'" where it openly speaks that the US Department of Defense is investing in technology to make its soldiers stronger and more agile. Again, this technology comes from prosthetics of people with disabilities.

It is not just the US that is investing in this technology. Russia and China are also in the match.

This prosthesis causes soldiers to run faster, to be more agile, but, above all, to carry more weight. In addition to all the equipment they need to carry in battle that weighs almost 60 kg, they are also capable of lifting obstacles, missiles and any other necessary object without getting tired.

The British site Express in its August 2018 issue published a story entitled "US announces mysterious 12 million pound experiments to create 'bio-reinforced' super-soldiers," commenting that "according to Department of Defense documents, bio-enhancement experiments will develop technologies to maximize physiological performances. This includes increased endurance, increased tolerance to environmental extremes, increased senses, and improved overall fitness without noticeable increase. Experimental objectives also hope to produce soldiers who need a fraction of the typical amount of sleep and who can handle highly stressful situations. "

Have you heard this somewhere?

But the worst is not that. The article continues, revealing that "one of these projects was to create software that could be loaded directly into the brain to give its soldiers more intense senses while also trying to cure diseases such as blindness, paralysis and speech disorders." Will it not be possible, in addition to all these benefits, to control emotions and suppress feelings? Practically robotic human beings. The perfect soldier: no emotions and questioning.

Just as Daniel had been trained to be.

CHAPTER **9**

ONE MISSION AFTER ANOTHER

Daniel and his world-class companions worked hard. They embarked on consecutive missions, most often with absolute success. As time passed by, many countries were revisited for a variety of reasons, including South Africa and the Netherlands, but the main one was Qatar. Not only for its strategic location in the Middle East, on the edge of the Persian Gulf, but also for harboring one of the major American bases in the world, located west of the capital Doha.

The visits to the base took place approximately three times a year, and the procedure was very similar. The US military base airport – not listed on the map – has two large lanes parallel to each other with a hangar in the middle, covered with darkened glass, which prevents anyone outside to see what happens inside. Inside, there is a door with a sign saying, "restricted access," where Daniel and his group passed.

After entering, they came across a very large escalator, bigger than a conventional one that we see in malls and airports, both in height and width. In addition to the size difference, the speed was also striking because it was much faster than the conventional one.

At the base of this escalator is a reception room where credentials are checked. After the entrance, there is another door (all very reinforced and with different types of security) that leads to a shed where different military vehicles can be seen and a room to the troops to remove its equipment – like a dressing room. Everyone gets undressed and uniforms are delivered. At the exit of the "locker room" you can see some training rooms and laboratories to which everyone should go.

The first visit is to the medical examination room, where everyone only wears shorts and receives a tape that will be stuck in the arm for the whole time at the base with personal information relevant to the exams. There, as soon as they arrive, a scraping of the skin is already done, and the content taken to study. This entire examination process takes approximately three hours.

After checking that everyone is well, they return to the locker room, take a shower, change uniforms again and are taken to the military camp, west of the base.

Between missions, Daniel and his companions are always in training. In the case of this American base in Qatar, it's focused on survival in the desert. The heat is too high. So terrible that it makes the soldiers hallucinate sometimes, also due to deprivation of water. When they are not in specific training, they all exercise and assist in base safety patrol.

The call comes from a siren a bit different from the conventional ones and the soldiers must appear in the runway of the airplanes in an hour. On the aircraft door they receive the mission summary that will be executed. Intervention missions with guerrillas in the region's wars (Iran, Iraq, Saudi Arabia, Yemen, etc.) were very common, including acting as instructors for local army members in each country.

DAY OFF

In rare moments of rest, usually after more complicated or controversial missions (such as encounters with non-humans), Daniel was sent back to Brazil to rest and with money to enjoy his "vacations". Always in military flight, never in conventional airplanes.

Apart from the time with the family, he used to spend a month in his country home applying to short vocational courses and sometimes even a few temporary jobs. On a certain visit, he stayed with his family for three months, working as a security guard at a local bingo.

When inside the bases, it was common to work for two days and to rest one.

STRAY BULLET

On one of the visits to the American military base in Qatar, a specific siren for his troops was fired and they all moved to the plane. Arriving there, they were given the description of their mission, which was to map a certain area in Jordan where there could be artifacts that were of great interest to the command. The task was to map, locate and warn the position to the base.

They then flew to a military base in the destination country and headed towards the Dead Sea on the border with Israel. The area they were covering was about 400 meters away from the water, in a place full of canyons, cracks and caves.

About 100 elite world troopers patrolled the entire region with the help of a local guide. They traversed the cracks and about nineteen caves, finding many curious "artifacts," and their location was immediately sent to the central command.

One of the discoveries caught Daniel's attention. It was a sort of golden ship buried in the crevices of a canyon. It was not possible to see very well because of the sand, but it was certainly something different and great that attracted a lot of attention. But since they were not there to ask questions, they did their job and moved on.

As they were walking back to the nearby vehicles to make their way to the base, one of the colleagues standing next to Daniel fell to the ground for no apparent reason. When they checked what had happened to the man lying on the floor, they could see a perforation in his head.

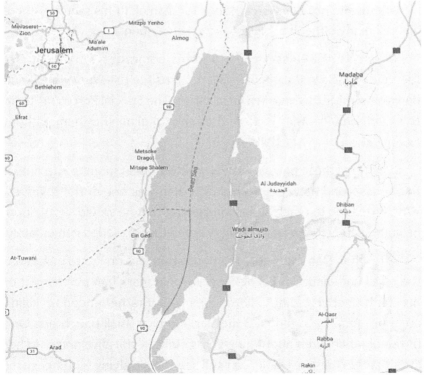

FIGURE 9: Mission area near the Dead Sea between Israel and Jordan (right).

As there was no apparent conflict nearby, it was concluded that it was a stray bullet. The projectile was from a 762 rifle, very common in the region. Fortunately, the bullet did not hit his brain, it went through the soldier's helmet and lodged in his skull. He was rushed to the local base where he was treated successfully.

After medical care, they all returned to Qatar base once more on the CS Lockheed military aircraft.

REPENTANCE IN BOSNIA

Things did not always work out for Daniel. In his memory there are still many difficult to digest facts; consequences of war.

In one of the missions, he and his comrades were behind a faction of rebels in Bosnia. They were Serbs fugitive, very violent and dangerous, trying to hide in a local village. The Special Force was there to search and kill, that is, to find them and eliminate them without any question.

On one of these patrols, Daniel spotted a man running into one of the houses, and he was sure that this man was one of the fugitives. With little time to react, already imagining that he would shoot soon, he immediately threw an incendiary bomb that exploded immediately.

After that, Daniel entered the house that was on fire to make sure the rebel had died, but his discovery would mark him for the rest of his life: his action did not kill the enemy, but rather ended up killing an entire family – a father, a mother and two small daughters. One of the older children about nine years old was still alive and held her little sister in her lap. Daniel can still see the girl dying with her sister in her arms.

His training has always been: shoot first, ask questions later. Any mistake or hesitation on his part could cost him his life in a war. He knew all this. But this time it was hard to forget what he had done.

SKY LIGHTS

Still in Bosnia, the elite team received a wake-up call on unidentified lights that were flying over the military base in Zenica, the central region of the country. The sightings were confirmed by several civilians in the region and the population was already beginning to ask questions.

All the soldiers of the troop, including Daniel, moved there and spent about five days investigating what was happening both on the bases and in the surrounding cities.

In addition to a few confirmed sightings, several reports claimed that UFOs directed a kind of light into people, which left physical marks on their bodies. Some witnesses even said that it took some of the people's blood.

After five days of investigation, they were called back to base – even at the insistence of the frightened local population, who called for their help. Unable to help more, they returned. But not before they saw a luminous disk in the sky, which was about 60 meters wide, alternating its colors between red, blue, green and yellow, after a few moments, disappearing to be no longer seen.

The curious thing is that the ship did not flew up the sky as expected; it went down as if it entered the earth by some cleft to disappear.

HORRORS OF WAR

In one of the missions in Bosnia, the troops marched south of the capital Sarajevo. Passing one of the river bridges that cuts through the city, towards the local mountains, they could see that there were several bodies along the way. The result of several Serbian massacres in the region.

Sometimes they observed that not all these people were dead. Some were still dying in the ditches. They, unfortunately, could not stop to help, but they always called the Red Cross to help the wounded.

The bodies were not just ordinary civilians. Many ditches contained dead soldiers from various countries. The rebels bludgeoned the area, stealing weapons, ammunition and food from UN soldiers, including Russians, and then killing them.

Another curious undisclosed fact noted by Daniel is that the Serb rebels also killed several reporters and members of the press, but this action was never divulged as it happened.

THE REAL REASON FOR THE PRESENCE IN IRAQ

Undoubtedly, Iraq occupies a strategic geographical position in the world. In the middle of the Middle East, between the European continent and the Asian continent. In addition, it is a major oil producer – with large reserves – as well as being part of a large pipeline network leading from the Persian Gulf and neighboring countries – such as Kuwait – to the Mediterranean Sea (through Syria).

This already seems like a good reason to justify the war with Iraq, but it is not the main reason.

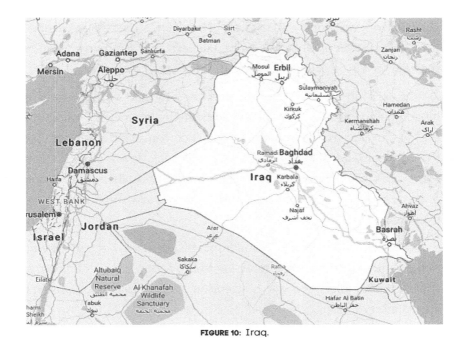

FIGURE 10: Iraq.

Locating, mapping and supporting the extraction of ancient devices that were underground. That is what most Daniel's missions were like, all depending on the intereses of the "secret command".

The most impressive mission located an artifact about one kilometer long in the middle of the Iraqi desert. Daniel did not know what that machine was, whether it was an aircraft or something, but its size frightened everyone. It took about six full months to remove about a quarter of it from the sand – due to its size, weight, depth and the concealment level. Some activities extended the mission, such as the blockade of air space in the region and the interception of troops that came very close to the ship.

The work was done with the help of intraterrestrial beings, because the manipulation of what was being taken from the region was done through specific DNA, which we did not have.

Daniel's job was to secure the perimeter by land, with the help of his companions. In addition, he should clean the perimeter. Sometimes they had to face troops from the UN itself or from allied countries (like the US itself), because the troops did not back down. In fact, there were cases in which soldiers (friend fire) and press (with apprehension of the equipment) – that arrived at the site and saw too much – were executed.

Iraq was divided into 237 quadrants by the allies. Each piece was ranked with a distinct color, referring to the action to be done on the spot. For example: yellow was attention and red was the signal for armed intervention.

The whole country has been and still is looted. This is the true interest in the region. They (secret government) have not needed oil for a long time.

Something curious remained in Daniel's mind throughout his visit to the region: if the place was heavily monitored and the war easily won, how did the rebels have armaments and supplies? How was it possible that this would enter the country with all the existing border c.

CHAPTER **10**

ANTARCTICA

Daniel has visited Antarctica three times, but the first time he set foot on the icy continent was in 1997. He and his comrades left the famous American military base in Qatar and headed to the island of Madagascar on the African continent where they stayed for two days. They took a plane to Australia and then a direct flight to Antarctica.

The first stop was a secret Russian military base, located near the official Vostok station, at the center of the East Antarctic Ice Sheet. They stayed on that base for approximately ten days in lodgings that looked like large containers. Some achieved around 82ft of width, 114ft of height and 164ft of lendth. The entire facility was underground, camouflaged by snow and painted white. From the outside you would see only an antenna that was also painted white, including its support cables, which made it practically undetectable.

After this period of acclimatization and ice training at the Russian base, they headed to the McMurdo American station, on the south tip of Ross Island in the New Zealand-claimed territory. They would spend the next twenty days there on a mission in the Transantarctic Mountains, which were nearby.

The main mission was to secure the perimeter for a gathering that would involve eight people, among scientists and military, in a confidential location in the middle of the mountains.

The Special Forces' mission was to search and secure within a five kilometer radius from the designated location. At each kilometer of the first three outside the secure region perimeter, the group built an electronic ring and an inner one of military troops. Inside the two kilometers inside the perimeter, security was done every 500 meters and the last ring, to which Daniel belonged, was only 350 meters from the center.

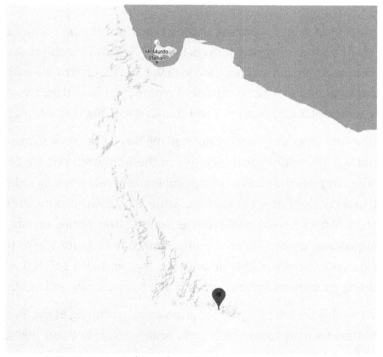

FIGURE 11: McMurdo (above) and the Transantarctic Mountains.

The curious thing is that this time the weapons were different. These were non-conventional laser weapons, for which they had received training at the base. No one was talking about it, but they all looked a little shocked for handling something so out of their everyday reality.

The pre-event briefing delivered to then said that they would not have major problems that day, because the meeting would involve "good" entities, coming from inner Earth.

The clouds were very low that day. Because of that it was difficult to verify if the entities would come from above. At one point, Daniel spotted a large white ship emerging from the clouds. It was very big and this image immediately scared everyone who was on the perimeter. The ship was about 800 meters long and because of the clouds it was impossible to see its end. The height was unimaginable. Daniel felt scared at the moment, but he needed to focus on his mission.

The ship landed, and from its main door two tall beings appeared. They had a very white skin, white hair and intensely blue eyes – much bigger than human eyes. Daniel watched with his binoculars.

As they left the ship, one of the creatures looked in the platoon's direction and waved bringing his hand to his chest. At that very moment, everyone – without exception, assumed a rest position: one knee on the floor, the other knee flexed (foot flat on floor), with the weapons crossing the chest. They stayed like this, without moving, for about three hours. They did not feel pain or fatigue, but they couldn't move. The body did not respond.

Seeing the panic that increased among the soldiers, the creature again turned to them and, as if talking to each one of then inside their minds, said: "Be calm, do not be afraid, nothing will happen to you". The sight was scary: 150 men kneeling and paralyzed at the same time.

At the end, the creatures entered the ship and disappeared in the clouds. At that moment everyone could stand up and wondered what happened.

Daniel repeated to himself that everything was fine, but deep down, the idea that there is a race in the universe that can control us that way, without any effort, was frightening.

Then, they all returned to McMurdo's American station for further mission interrogations and medical examinations. It was the first time that Daniel stayed at the station, and he already felt like home. He knew every corner – official and unofficial.

MCMURDO

McMurdo is an official United States station in Antarctica. Anyone can Google it and see the city with streets, houses and everything.

What Daniel tells us is what we can not see.

Just behind the barrels in the south of the city there is an entrance to the basement. The building is called "C3A" and has restricted access. After the stairs, we can see a laboratory and a large room that has a kind of cinema. There, Daniel and his comrades were trained and received missions' data.

FIGURE 12: McMurdo station and barrels in the south.

The last time Daniel was there, he received instructions in that place about the entities they could find on missions. One of them attracted a lot of attention and would end up being one of the worst encounters that he ever had.

THE GUARDIANS OF THE ICE

McMurdo's American station was the site of specific training against these entities. The first time he was there, Daniel spent a week in intense training for an eventual encounter. These trainings happened in rooms with 3D simulation technology (with virtual glasses) that simulated the encounters and all possible reactions of both parties.

These creatures were described by Daniel as a strange combination of a gorilla and a large dog. They are large – about 1.80 m tall, intelligent, have thick skin, are white and have very blue eyes, which makes difficult for then to see in the region because of ice and snow.

The information that they received in the training is that these creatures were artificially created by the Nazis between the 30s and 40s of the last century, brought to Antarctica – where the 3rd Reich (which would become the 4th Reich) already had a base. These creatures were trained to serve as the first baseman's defense against unwanted visits.

They are extremely violent entities, very strong, agile and difficult to detect in the region. Added to that, they possess considerable mental power, although they seem to be unaware of what they protect, for they have sometimes even paralyzed some soldiers they encountered in combat, before killing or kidnapping them. In the second case, no one ever came back to tell the story.

These beings are spread over a very large geographical area, protecting basically four bases from the 4th Reich. They form a barrier around the region. Antarctica is divided by the earthly and non earthly community into quadrants, according to the cities and bases below the ice.

There are several cities and bases below the Antarctic ice. Cities in our own molds, with streets, rails, buildings, ships and everything else we can imagine.

In the year 2017 there was the last conference between human beings and non-human entities with presence on the planet to discuss this geographical division of the continent and also discuss the perimeter of each one, to ensure that everyone would have an honest division and privacy.

FIGURE 13: Approximate Representation of the Creature (Movie The Mummy 3 – Universal / 2008).

THE ENCOUNTER

Daniel's first and only encounter with this creature was not at all pleasant, as we might have expected.

Daniel and his comrades were at the McMurdo's station when they were called to the famous briefing, that is, the detailing of the mission that was to come. This time, the instruction was to investigate, from a distance, the activities that took place at one of the secret bases of the 4th Reich which was located in the west of the Norwegian territory, known as the Queen Maud Land, in the local mountains.

The few men who were assigned to this mission – about thirty – went by helicopter a few miles away from the place and went from there on foot. To the naked eye, nothing was seen in the snow, nor in the mountains. But everyone knew that something could happen at any moment.

The command secured the perimeter of the area and positioned itself for observation. After about an hour on the spot, one of them caught the attention from others on the radio because of a suspicion of something moving between the ice. It was when, from a distance and through binoculars, Daniel watched one of the creatures fiercely approach the companion with a bite so powerful that it ripped off his head and threw it away, then dismembered the rest of his body.

Immediately they all backed away and retreated. At the moment, Daniel still had time to see from a distance a human about 1, 90 m, blond, white and with strong physic, behaving as if he were a commander. Fortunately, this was the only casualty of the meeting, but on their way out, they still saw several of these creatures prowling the troop as if they wanted to make sure they were leaving and would not come back.

CHAPTER 11

THE LAST MISSION

Daniel and his companions were again at the military base in Qatar when they received a message announcing their displacement to Somalia. 2003 was the year and the destination base was located near the Mandera triangle (where the countries of Somalia, Ethiopia and Kenya meet), region that was controlled by the Americans but officially belonged to NATO forces.

Their mission in Somalia was to recognize the area, as there were suspicions that non-human entities – more specifically those known as reptilians and grays – were operating in the area without authorization.

When that happens, it was usually related to the abduction of humans.

On that base all the command received a more confrontational training about these entities. After all the instructions, they proceeded to the designated region – further into the Somali territory, south of the city of Doolow.

Every morning, soldiers took a shot of alcohol (usually vodka) to deal with infections in that inhospitable environment.

This time it was no different. After the traditional morning shot on the third day of patrolling, they all marched into the desert area early in the morning. Around six o'clock, their commander received a radio warning that a UN convoy traveling to Kenya would have to pass through the region and their assistance was necessary to secure the border near the city of Mandera.

The troop then stopped and waited for the train. There were about ninety heavily armed men on foot. If they needed help, they would radio the helicopters for rescue, and everything else was done on the ground and without motor vehicles.

A few hours later, five trucks arrived carrying wooden boxes covered with a brown tarp, looking like groceries or something of that sort. As expected, no one asked.

Since it was not possible for the five trucks to give a ride to the ninety soldiers who escorted them, the entire convoy followed the march of the troops at 5 km / h, who had ten of their men in the trucks and the rest marching, taking turns from time to time.

FIGURE 14: The Mandera triangle in Eastern Africa where the countries of Kenya, Ethiopia, and Somalia meet.

A few minutes of displacement in this rhythm passed, Daniel sighted with his binoculars – while in the truck – a movement that happened at a distance. They checked the equipment and the satellite did not show anything for some reason. The suspicion was of a fire or something of the sort, but the fog prevented the vision in the occasion.

That was when Daniel realized that it was a group of people coming in the opposite direction – probably refugees from the Melkadida or Kobe camps in Ethiopia. The estimative was of five hundred people. Immediately Daniel communicated the sighting to the troop after giving them the cry of attention.

Immediately, the operation's commander – a major from the American army – requested formation to the elite troops directly of the second truck of the convoy. From there, he called Daniel, who was in the truck ahead, to stand beside him. Immediately, all the trucks leaned against each other, locking each other and forming something like a locomotive.

Daniel and the Major stood on the trunk of the trucks watching the troop forming on the ground and the crowd approaching. Daniel thought at that moment that he had only two things to do: shoot everyone, which would be absurd for several reasons, or push everyone to stay away from the train and the soldiers. The second option was given as an order.

At the meeting with the multitude of refugees, the troop in formation pushed and moved the people coming towards them. So, the Major, from above the truck, picked up a bamboo stick that protected the side of one of the trucks. With it, he began to beat people walking beside the truck where he was.

Daniel did not understand what the Major was doing and politely asked him to calm down. The Major did not even look back and kept pounding. Daniel suspected that the commander of the operation was under the influence of narcotics, for his behavior was not normal, much less his physiognomy.

It was then that the bamboo stick with which the major hit the people hit an eye of a child, who was in the lap of his mother, certainly blinding her. Not satisfied yet, he also hit the mother with the instrument. Daniel, seeing the situation, could not contain himself and elbowed the major, causing him to fall into the cover and causing the bamboo to fall out of the truck.

Immediately, the Major drew his pistol and pointed it at Daniel, giving him a jail sentence. Daniel then took out his pistol, pointed it at the major, and said, "shoot!" He realized that the major was not in full control of his actions and did not hesitate, firing at the commander more than nine times.

Daniel lost his balance, hit the corner of the truck and fell backwards on the ground, losing his breath from the impact. At that moment, he noticed a bite on the right side of his neck and then another bite on the left side, which should be morphine or any other soothing substance that made him faint immediately.

PRISONER

Daniel awoke hours later in a plane, not knowing his destination and without having anyone to ask. He was in an armchair, with a seat belt buckled, alone at the bottom of the aircraft.

Minutes later they landed on the edge of the Mediterranean Sea in the city of Marseilles in southern France. Daniel was then taken to a Foreign Legion barracks, where he spent about a week. He was treated very well, but he could not get information on what was happening. No one there knew why he had been arrested or what his fate would be.

During this time in Marseilles, Daniel found a sergeant with whom he had been on a mission a few years earlier. As the missions' comrades changed much from one to another, it is not very common to find people in the displacements. The former colleague had no information on why Daniel was there and did not know what the next steps would be. Unfortunately, he had no access to information. Apparently, the same situation served for everyone in the barracks.

His cell was comfortable. It was about 4.5 m x 4.5 m and had a bathroom and shower with hot water, a coffee table or reading table, television, newspapers and magazines – all in French, which did not help much, but it was distracting at times. In addition, he was entitled to daily sunbathing. Over time, he became friends with the staff of the barracks and began to participate in physical activities with the local squad, sometimes even giving instructions on armaments and tactics.

After a week in Marseilles, Daniel was transferred to countless prisons around the world. He first spent about twenty days in Algeria, then in a barracks near Rome, Italy, shortly after going to a prison in Corsica, to return to Marseilles and spend another month there. He was then arrested in another city off the coast of France to be transferred to a barracks in Gibraltar near the English navy docks when he was finally transferred to South America. He spent 15 days imprisoned in French Guiana. After that, he spent a week in Suriname and was transferred to a barracks in Manaus (jungle operation). From there, he was imprisoned in several places in Brazil including Bahia, Rio de Janeiro, but mainly in the Rio Grande barracks, in the state of Rio Grande do Sul.

In total, they were eight months in jail, traveling around the world. During this time, all his friends and family received visits from local authorities, and Daniel obviously had no idea. These "visits" were police raids – usually a Brazilian federal police delegate, following two or more unidentified foreign agents – who turned people's houses up and down, looking for pictures, letters, computers, and any documents they sent to them that proved that Daniel served the Special Forces. Even some intimidation was revealed.

Later, this whole process would generate many problems for Daniel in his daily life. Many relatives did not want to talk to him, friends disappeared and even the mother of his daughter at the time cut off relations with him. His job would charge that price of him.

CHAPTER 12

BACK HOME

When he was released from Rio Grande barracks, Daniel went to Porto Alegre and was taken by bus to Brasilia, where his family lives. A long trip, in which he could reflect on several moments of these last years and think about what would be of his life now. He was always a warrior, a soldier. The uncertainty of the future bothered him.

After arriving in the capital of Brazil, he landed at the bus station. He picked up a cab that left him at the door of his house (or what he believed to be his home). To his surprise, it was not. He rang the bell and a lady answered the door. Daniel apologized and left. He could not remember his home address. A strange new sensation of not knowing where he was, even though he felt at home in the city he knew as the back of his hand. It was then that he went to a payphone and phoned his father, who promptly went to get him at the address where Daniel was at that moment.

The first days at home were very difficult. Despite all the support received from his father and mother, he saw his brother and the rest of the family turning their backs on him, avoiding conversation. Sometimes Daniel could listen to conversations where they called him a liar and accusing him of living a double life and that they were all victims. Besides, that house – the one he'd grown up – did not look familiar. It was as if he were in a strange place.

As if that were not enough, he noticed that he had memory lapses. Often, when he left the house, he forgot where he was going. At other times he could not remember the way back. A simple trip to the market could take hours or an entire day. By the way, to this day, Daniel still stops in the street to remember his way and its destiny.

Daniel used to sleep when he could, about two or three hours a night. He would often lie down on bed and think about life, about things he went through, and about what he was going to do.

On one of those nights, he began to wonder why he was having memory lapses. He could not understand how he might be suffering from it if he always had a clear and fast mind. Until one day he could remember some things that could explain what was going on with him.

The first thing was about his period in Marseilles. There were some interrogations about his missions and his work, but shortly thereafter he was placed in a comfortable, reclined chair with a device that came down to his head – like a beauty salon chair – that would surely be used to erase his memoirs.

FIGURE 15: Salon chair like that used to erase memories.

Continuing his thoughts, he managed to remember more things. Whenever there were missions where the troop encountered nonhuman entities, they went through the same "chair" process – certainly to erase their memories. Many times, he recalled, all the combatants used to leave the labs staggering with fatigue and sleep, going straight to their rooms to sleep for long periods thereafter.

Daniel could not believe he had not remembered it until then. It was further proof that this technology had been used. Along with his war memories, a few other things went away, such as his ability to swim and even how to handle a parachute, things that were once daily and now became something unheard of for his mind. It was impressive for him to think how many times he had gone through this process in all the years he served, but now he could see all its effects.

CHAPTER **13**

TECHNOLOGIES FOR THE MINORITY

In The Ascension Mysteries (2016), David Wilcock, author and researcher, describes his conversations with one of his informants named Pete Peterson.

Pete comes from a very interesting family. His grandfather was the right-hand man of Nicola Tesla (1853-1943), a Serbian inventor and certainly one of the greatest geniuses that ever existed on this planet.

David says that in one of his conversations, Pete confirms that the supersonic frequency of television can be modified to attract the attention of viewers and that more than eight different strategies are being used to manipulate people subliminally every day – among them the famous NLP, or Neuro Linguistic Programming. One of the examples he mentions is the "obey and consume" message being exposed in a video where the eyes can not pick up the message, but the information is taken directly into the subconscious.

This technology has a history of being used in various media, not only on television, but also in music, radio and the advertising market in general, including the exploration of archetypes – figures or images that talk directly with the human subconscious.

This technique is not only used in the general population, but also in the military, and was certainly used in Daniel. All this so that he executed his mission with precision and without emotions, and so that he forgot the facts after his obligation had finished.

CONSCIOUS X SUBCONSCIOUS

The human mind is really fascinating. It is basically divided into three parts: the unconscious, the subconscious and the conscious.

The unconscious is the part that takes care of the automatic and involuntary functions of the body, like the breathing, the heart beats, the digestion, among others. In addition, it controls the immune system and related functions.

The conscious is that part of the mind that remains awake and focused on the present. Always worried about solving the problem immediately, being very rational, analytical and responsible for the will power. Its main function is to analyze the fastest way to solve the problem that is presented to you at the moment, without worrying about future consequences. There are stored the short-term memories. Being quick and objective, the conscious does not like repetitions or very long and lengthy information. Communication should be quick and accurate.

The subconscious is where our long-term emotions, habits, and memories meet. A feature of the subconscious is to look for the easiest way to solve long-term problems, taking into account your lifelong knowledge (or lives) and focusing on our self-preservation. The subconscious likes repetitions and slow and frequent communications.

We call the "Critical Factor of Mind" any suggestion that can pass the barrier of the conscious and access the unconscious without being rejected. This analysis is based on the person's belief and experience. If it asserts what the unconscious already knows, it is accepted. If the new information comes against your beliefs, it is rejected.

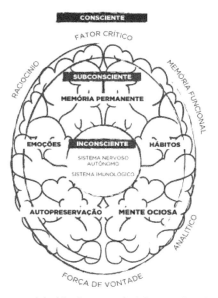

FIGURE 16: model of the human mind. Source: Gerald Kein.

In the case of subliminal information or communication techniques, the attempt is to dribble the conscious mind – through information that is not grasped by the conscious mind – and are delivered, captured and absorbed directly by the unconscious.

The problem is that these messages are "orders" that are given to us and that are related to what we like, want and seek from the beginning. The example of "obeying" and "consuming" given by Wilcock is great, because in both cases our mind accepts and likes the suggestions, because they are actions that make us feel good, accepted and happy by the way we were created according to the functioning of society.

Since the subconscious loves a repetition, the fact that it is repeated extensively does not bother us, on the contrary. We feel good every time we have this statement. This all comes back to us like endorphin, serotonin and other chemical rewards the brain gives us. This closes the cycle that reinforces the success of these suggestions and perpetuates our submission to those who control us – whether military (as in Daniel's case) or not.

SECRET SPACE PROGRAM

In 1947, the term "flying saucer" was created after American military man Kenneth Arnold spotted an Unidentified Flying Object (UFO) in his search for one of his lost planes in a battle exercise. Later, in an interview, he used the term that would be immortalized.

Soon after this event, we had the famous case of the city of Roswell in the United States. We can say that it is the first case of sighting and contact with extraterrestrials officially registered in human history – if we analyze only the traditional media and science, obviously.

Roswell was basically a crash of a flying saucer, where bodies of its crew were found, and all this was sighted and witnessed by local citizens. The fact was even published on the front pages of local newspapers the next day, to be discredited soon after, when the military said it was a "weather balloon."

After World War II (1938-1945), the United States implemented a project called "Operation Paperclip". It consisted of hiring all the scientists who headed the Nazi organization of Adolf Hitler to be key players in the country's development, especially in aerospace technologies. It is no wonder that the leading scientist, Wenher Von Braun (1912-1977) was chief of NASA for several years, including actively participating in the Apollo missions, which took the man to the moon in July 1969.

FIGURE 17: Von Braun in the upper circle and Adolf Hitler in the center with the Nazi leadership in 1933 (Source: anecdotes-spatiales.com).

What is beneath this operation is the transfer of technology from flying saucers, widely known by Nazi Germany. After the War were found several prototypes and planes of aircraft with technology much more advanced than the others at the time. William Tompkins, a retired aerospace engineer, says he participated in the creation of the Secret Space Program and also studied documents on antigravity vehicles developed by Nazis in World War II.

Speaking on NASA's Apollo missions, one of his 14th astronauts ended up being one of the biggest whistleblowers (Edgar Mitchell). He openly said that the Roswell case was true and that humanity had been in contact with the aliens for decades.

In the same context, a former Canadian defense minister (from 1963 to 1967) Paul Hellyer, now 96 years old (2019), still says that governments have contact with at least four alien races.

Since then the subject of a secret space force has been exclusively being discussed by so-called "conspiracy theorists" until the year 2019. In February of that year, Donald Trump, the President of the United States, signed the term creating an American Military Space Forces SPD-4), making official what has been said for years.

Now, we ask you. Why would we need a space force if an extraterrestrial force were not known?

David Wilcock, in the aforementioned "Ascension Mysteries", comments on his informant codenamed Jacob. He would be a high-ranking former military man who would have presented irrefutable evidence about the existence of a secret space program since World War II. He is just one among so many who are coming to the public with impressive information. Wilcock studies each one in depth; It is worth reading.

COREY GOODE

Nowadays it is practically impossible to speak in Secret Space Program or any subject related to extraterrestrials and not to speak of Corey Goode. The former American IT professional claims to have been trained as a child as an apprentice, to finally be abducted to work on a program called "20 and back".

This program would consist of twenty years of work for the Secret Space Program in various functions, then having its memory erased, its physical body chemically regressed to the initial appearance and put back at the time of abduction, through regression in time through a special machine that performs this function.

Yes, this is very confusing. Corey says he went through this experience three times, that is, it served sixty years to the program. If you want to know more, look for his website and know his story in the "Cosmic Disclosure" program on TV Gaia. Here we will mention only a few things of what he says about the extraterrestrial presence on Earth.

When he finally returned from the program with the secret space service, Corey reported intriguing encounters with extraterrestrials on our planet. According to him, they are intra-terrestrial beings, that is, they live inside the crust of the Earth.

In one of his stories, he describes a woman named A'ree, who ends up developing a friendship with him and even a certain affection, since a ceremony of openness of mind, if I may so call it, was performed between them.

He describes several visits to this breed, and also mentions that they would not be the only ones present here. Among those cited, several races of reptilians, insectoids and the famous "avians" who, according to him, are their guides and protectors.

Corey also mentions that in his time of service in the space command he had access to various technologies. Many of them are similar to the ones Daniel describes on his journey. One is the so-called "smart glasses" or tablets (we're talking about the early 90's!). This was almost unimaginable at the time if it were not the science-fiction films and series, like Star Trek, which already presented such an idea to the public.

DAVID ICKE AND EMERY SMITH

We can not fail to mention two interesting figures on the question of the extraterrestrial presence on Earth.

The first is David Icke. The British former footballer has been ridiculed for most of his life for claiming that aliens are on Earth and more: they control a hidden government.

Icke is going through a new phase today. With the information being released to the public recently, several theories he has commented on for years are being revealed as true. He has several books published and, in addition, he does several lectures around the world.

Emery Smith is a new figure on the set, but very intriguing. He is a veteran of the US Air Force who claims to have been a coroner on secret bases, working side by side with non-human beings and doing autopsies on thousands of extraterrestrial bodies.

He also describes in TV Gaia's "Cosmic Disclosure" series, with rich detail, his experiences of working side by side with these beings and the impression he has on them. There were dozens of alien species that were partners of the military.

HUMAN TECHNOLOGY

Several patents related to the aerospace industry are registered every year. In addition, with the laws of the United States that guarantee the population's access to documents that are more than 50 years old, some intriguing projects are revealed. Not to mention those released by Edward Snowden and Wikileaks.

Now, I would like to discuss some information from the Brazilian Ufo Review, in its April 2019 virtual edition, written by Mel Polidori, titled "American Navy has secretly designed a reverse technology craft."

The report says that through a US patent analysis, it is possible to say that the military presented plans to build an aircraft that "uses an inertial mass reduction device to travel at extreme speeds."

It is certainly an extremely complex technology for the common mind, but it is supposed to use gravitational waves. The curiosity is that these waves were discovered only in 2016, when we observed the collision between two black holes. This means that, through the electromagnetic force, the craft creates a kind of vacuum around itself, eliminating all resistance and causing the vehicle to reach enormous speeds, and can be used in air, water or sidereal space – as described in the patent itself.

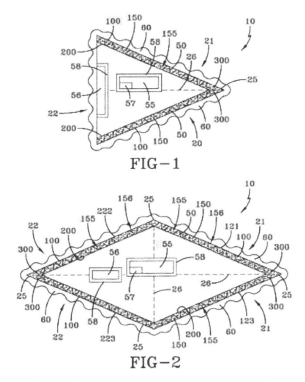

FIGURE 18: Original drawings of the patent. Source: Salvatore Cezar Pais / Google.

The report also mentions U.S. Pentagon UFO research projects, which requested information on 38 different projects including "antigravity, invisibility, space fold engine and wormhole" technologies, among other unconventional propulsion methods.

All of these patents have already been released until 2018. There are no confirmations that the aircraft have been manufactured and tested, but there are reports of sightings that meet the characteristics mentioned in the projects described above.

You see, this is an official US Navy record, not a conspiracy theory or science fiction movie script. It is not a matter of wanting to believe or have faith in something. It's about reality, whether you accept it or not.

What Daniel lived and felt on his skin for over twenty years is beginning to be revealed now.

CHAPTER **14**

OUTBURST OF A SOLDIER

This chapter was written by Ted Heidt – the "Daniel" of real life.

Iraqi's most recent armed invasion, the British-American coalition became responsible for international crimes. The qualification of aggression as crime against peace leaves no doubt; in addition to that, the practice of war crimes and crimes against humanity can be easily demonstrated. However, the international condemnation was extremely shy, and the fight against impunity for such crimes, while much desired ad hoc by international jurisdiction, it appears politically difficult to happen. This leads us, more than ever, to rethink international law and the organization of the international community around the question of justice against British-American troops.

There is no doubt that the crimes of the Anglo-American coalition are an attack to fundamental interests of the international community and an influence on the conscience of all humanity (and mobilization from public opinion confirms this!). For this reason, these crimes raise a debate about the absolute necessity of imperative norms in international law and about denunciation and repression of these odious crimes. Through these measures, in the future, the repetition of such acts will be less and less tolerable and increasingly uncomfortable to the Americans and British people.

In times of balance of the human victims and other damages caused by the military operations of the Anglo-American coalition, there are people who claim that we have reached a post-war period. However, this refers to a specific post-war period: free Iraq. But the postwar period cannot be limited to humanitarian aid and the reconstruction of Iraq; it must also create conditions for justice to the Iraqi's people and the international community. A lasting peace in the region cannot prevent this phase of fight against impunity for all the international crimes. That is, both the crimes committed by the Iraqi authorities in the last decades and those perpetrated by the Anglo-American coalition in what must be called, as Sami Nair calls, a "colonial invasion". Without justice being done, revenge will inevitably take the form of terrorist acts, the last resort of the victims, condemned to do justice with their own hands. Justice also facilitates national reconciliation.

In recent years, several proposals on the crimes of the Iraqi regime have been made. One of them is the establishment of an international ad hoc tribunal, a solution recently reiterated by NGOs, including FIDH, which we can only approve. Since the Rome Statute, which established the international criminal court, provides that it has no retroactive effect (for acts prior to its entry into force on 1 July 2002).

On the crimes of the Anglo-American coalition the voices are more discreet, but not absent ([1]), illustration of this unsustainable policy of double standards. An example of this is the US ambassador's proposal on war crimes, which states that "the Security Council should also limit the Court's jurisdiction to the crimes of Iraqi officials and waste no time on dubious complaints about the coalition's behavior during the Gulf War and Operation Iraqi Freedom. The Security Council must make pragmatic decisions and this time things will run better".

It seems easier, or less uncomfortable, to report the crimes of the weakest. Let lawyers be allowed to waste time on these less and less dubious complaints in three ways: the qualification, conviction and repression of the crimes in question.

I. In order to classify the crimes, it is first necessary to qualify the acts committed by the coalition which are liable to give rise to legal liability.

1. The first crime committed, and the most serious for the stability of international relations, is undoubtedly the crime of aggression. The legal community agrees that the outbreak of Anglo-American hostilities is a violation of international law. Therefore, it cannot be based on Security Council resolution 1441. This means that it does not qualify as self-defense and cannot be characterized as a preemptive war – despite a study of my case in 1997 – which is a non-existent concept in international law. In a judgment of the Nuremberg Tribunal, on 30 September 1946, it can be read that "To initiate a war of aggression, therefore, is not only an international crime; it is the supreme international crime differing only from other war crimes that it contains within itself the accumulated evil of the whole". In the Corfu Channel case, the International Court regarded "the alleged right of intervention as the manifestation of a policy of force, has given right to the most serious abuses and as such cannot, whatever be the present defects in international organization, find a place in international law. Intervention is perhaps still less admissible in the particular form it would take here; for, from the nature of things, it would be reserved for the most powerful States, and might easily lead to perverting the administration of international justice itself."

The Definition of Aggression (established on the United Nations General Assembly Resolution 3314 on December 14, 1974, adopted by consensus and used later by the Code of Offences Against the Peace and Security of Mankind of The International Law Commission), in the present case of a direct military operation, it is indisputable: "Aggression is the use of armed force by a State against the sovereignty, territorial integrity or political independence of another State, or in any other manner inconsistent with the Charter of the United Nations". Articles on State Responsibility define aggression as an international crime: "aggression is the most serious and dangerous form of illegal use of force" (text of Res. 3314). The qualification of aggression's crime is important for the further execution of individual criminal responsibility.

2. The British-American coalition may also be responsible for war crimes. The information we have at the moment is partial, with the attackers doing everything they can so that there is only data that indicates a clean war. However, from a certain number of information, some conclusions can be drawn and should be submitted to an international commission of inquiry. The Coalition for the International Criminal Court issued a warning (made by approximately 100 jurists) – even before the outbreak of hostilities and in the light of the precedents from Gulf War and the campaigns in Kosovo and Afghanistan – to American and British leaders of the risk of war crimes charges.

Several violations of the fundamental rules of the law of war have been committed, specifically Articles 35, 48, 51, 52 and 53 of the Additional Protocol to the Geneva Conventions on the Protection of Victims of International Armed Conflicts (later, Protocol I). These Articles say that a conflict must, under any circumstances, differentiate military objectives from civilian objects and persons (they cannot be victims of attacks) and that disproportionate or indiscriminate means of attack cannot be used. The following non-exhaustive facts appear to constitute war crimes:

- Indiscriminate bombing of cities, such as the one that struck al-Hilla on April 1. According to the International Committee of the Red Cross, all the victims of this bombing were civilians. Also, the bombing of the Baghdad market on 26 March and the bombing of the residential neighborhood of Al-Mansour, also in Baghdad on 7 April, caused numerous civilian deaths and injuries;

- Two indiscriminate and disproportionate modes of attack: on the one hand, the "infernal column" advance used in Baghdad and in several southern cities by the US armor and on the other hand the practice of "search and kill", used by American marines to kill countless civilians without giving them a chance to surrender. Numerous civilian casualties were provoked without the possibility of surrender or after further appeals from front-line Special Forces to the Killer Troop (^{2}) who, at twilight, used their technologies and pulverized American troops stationed at barriers in Nadjaf and al-Hilla as a form of retaliation for indiscriminate actions against civilians. So, the coalition used that fact to increase its alert to terrorist acts by Iraqis or allies;

- The use of cluster bombs, as reported by the Red Cross representative in Iraq, as in Al-Hilla and Basra, denounced by Amnesty International (March 27, 2003 press release) and by Human Rights Watch (press release of 16 April 2003), contrary to Protocol I (article 51 [4] and 35 [2]), which prohibits "indiscriminate attacks" and those committed "in such a way as to cause unnecessary injury or suffering". Equally disregarded were Article 35, which establishes as a fundamental rule the principle of proportionality and Article

55 (1), which concerns the protection of the environment. The use of depleted uranium weapons, used massively during the first Gulf War (^{3}) and whose use in this campaign can be demonstrated is also contrary to Protocol I. These two categories of weapons are contrary to the United Nations Convention of 10 October 1980 and its Protocols on the prohibition or limitation of certain classical weapons that produce indiscriminate traumatic or triggering effects, as well as to the Ottawa Convention, which prohibits the use of anti-personnel mines;

- Attacks on civilian objects and infrastructure such as television bombings – described by Amnesty as war crimes in its communicated of March 26 – , attacks on ministries and administrative services, schools, places of worship, cultural heritage and indispensable supplies for the survival of civilian population, such as drinking water installations and irrigation works, leading to a serious humanitarian crisis for civilians. Several cities, such as Basra, were deprived of safe piped water and electricity almost two weeks after the outbreak of hostilities;

- Obstructions of the occupying forces to the work of humanitarian organizations, contrary to the requirements of articles 63, 142 and 143.5 of the Fourth Geneva Convention;

- Bombing of Palestine Hotel reaching journalists and facilities of the Arab jail Al Jazira, qualified by the International Federation of Journalists as "war crimes that cannot go unpunished" and leading to the request for an international inquiry;

- Regarding prisoners of war, the distinction Americans should have made between regular and unlawful combatants by denying to the unlawful ones the rights recognized by the Geneva Conventions, subjecting them to inhuman treatment or torture, as they had already done with the Guantánamo detainees after the war in Afghanistan; even the act of "willfully depriving a prisoner of war of the rights of fair and regular trial" constitutes a war crime under Article 8 of the Rome Statute.

- Possible assassinations of Iraqi soldiers who surrendered in Safouane, reported by the civilian population and one of the authors of this article. In addition to the above, killings of civilians after the end of hostilities that occurred during various protests against the Anglo-American occupation can also be qualified as war crimes for the excessive and disproportionate use of force.

3. The following acts may also be qualified as crimes against humanity:

- Situations of "deportation or forcible transfer of population" as recently defined in Article 7 (2) (d) of the Rome Statute: facts reported by humanitarian organizations demonstrate the existence of a plan pre-established by Kurdish forces shortly after taking over control of the Kirkuk region; members of the al-Shummar tribe left four villages of Kirkuk due to a written order given by a Kurdish official; as well as about 2,000 inhabitants of the villages of al-Muntasir, Khaid, al-Wahda and Umar Ibn al-Khattab, who were forced to leave their homes under armed threat while being dispossessed of their property. A Kurdish official said that this policy "was approved by the US and coalition forces". These acts also constitute a violation of Article 6 of the Fourth Geneva Convention, which requires the occupying forces to take action to prevent human rights abuses;

- Hypotheses of arrests and persecutions described in Article 7 (1) (e) and (h) of the Rome Statute, such as the prolonged or repeated detention of individuals due to their political, religious or cultural beliefs. Thus the will of the American authorities to keep some prisoners, including civilians and regular and unlawful combatants, under the pretext that they act against the command or belong to the Ba'ath party or to allegedly terrorist religious groups, leads to the serious denial of fundamental rights recognized by international law. These acts, which are henceforth qualified as war crimes, also fall under the category of crimes against humanity for discriminatory intent;

- Plunder or systematic destruction of monuments or buildings that belong to the Iraqi cultural heritage, from the moment they take place within the framework of a planned policy. In April, the National Library was burned down and the seven largest Iraqi national museums were plundered. Some published information suggests that this kind of plunder comes from a deliberate project by the occupation forces to steal the world's oldest civilization to the benefit of American and British art dealers:

(a) these plunders have always occurred in cities under the control of coalition forces. Witnesses report that the American cannons were standing outside the main entrance of the National Museum of Baghdad when the robbers emptied the museum in the face of the indifferent behavior of American soldiers.

(b) On 17 April, following the instructions of the UN General Secretary, the General Director of UNESCO organized a hearing in Paris to define strategies to be adapted. At the end of this meeting, one of the experts confirmed that professionalism in the execution of the looting indicates that "they were planned outside Iraq" and that ordinary citizens participated in them. Everything seems to indicate that the professionals of the art market have appropriated the most precious works.

(c) Finally, several eminent archaeologists have recently denounced a coalition between art dealers and American lawyers specializing in this type of trade: the American Council for Cultural Policy (ACCCP), which negotiated before the beginning of the conflict with the State Department and US Department of Defense a lightening of American and Iraqi legislation in order to facilitate the plundering of Iraqi historical heritage. The precedents that occurred during the Gulf War demonstrate the escape of numerous cultural works for English and American museums. It would not be the first time that the US and British military would commit international crimes; some studies have already reported war crimes committed during the first Gulf War. But so far this has never been officially denounced or condemned; and the international crimes committed by the conquering State were not repressed! When will we dare to take this step?

II. The condemnation of the crimes committed

1. To condemn a state for aggression seems to be "madness" in the current international scene, and in fact the crime of aggression is "the supreme international crime". The political organs have always been timid, only referring to the "rupture of international peace and security", including the invasion of Kuwait by Iraq, although in this case the term "invasion" was clearly assigned to the aggressor – contained in the first resolution adapted by the Security Council. In a second resolution of 6 August, it is stated that the Security Council is "Determined to bring the invasion and occupation of Kuwait by Iraq to an end and to restore the sovereignty, independence and territorial integrity of Kuwait" (resolution 661-1990).

In principle, the conviction should emanate from the United Nations Security Council, the main body responsible for maintaining peace and international security. But even if there is a blockade of the Security Council, as in this case – which undoubtedly took place through the United States and the United Kingdom – , there is another solution that is to hold an emergency session of the General Assembly. The Assembly recognized for itself, through resolution 377 (V), "the Union for the maintenance of peace", the responsibility to replace the Security Council in case of blockage.

The General Assembly recognize that the Council: "Resolves that if the Security Council, because of lack of unanimity of the permanent members, fails to exercise its primary responsibility to the maintenance of international peace and security in any case where there appears to be a threat to the peace, breach of the peace, or act of aggression, the General Assembly shall consider the matter immediately with a view to making appropriate recommendations to Members for the collective measures, including in the case of a breach of the peace or act of aggression the use of armed force when necessary, to maintain or restore international peace and security". The meeting in extraordinary session implies convocation by the Security Council with the favorable vote of 7 members or at the request of half of the members of the organization. There have been ten precedents on behalf of this resolution, on the question of Palestine.

In a press release issued on 18 March, the International Federation of Human Rights called for an emergency meeting of the General Assembly in accordance with resolution 377 (V) "to express its condemnation of the United States armed operation as constituting a flagrant violation of the Charter of the United Nations". This section was also requested by the Parliamentary Assembly of the Europe's Council and the League of Arab States.

In addition to the condemnation for rupture of peace, the organs belonging to the United Nations recall – sometimes by resolution – the international obligations of the belligerents to respect the Geneva Conventions and the generality of international humanitarian law. The Security Council has also denounced in several resolutions violations of international humanitarian law, as in the conflict between Iraq and Iran. In the case of the former Yugoslavia, the Security Council recalled respect for international humanitarian law by the parties, reiterated the principle of individual criminal responsibility (resolution 709 and 764 of 1992) and condemned violations of international humanitarian law (resolution 771 of 1992). The General Assembly even qualified some serious violations of the Geneva Convention on the Protection of Civilian Persons in Time of War as "war crimes" (resolution 46/47 A). On the occasion of the massacre of Palestinian civilians in the Sabra and Shatila refugee camps, they were characterized as a crime of "genocide," for which "the principals and accomplices – whether private individuals, public officials or statesmen, are punishable."

2. What happened to the US-British invasion of Iraq? Few reactions, no doubt! There was no resolution by the organs of the United Nations, nor the convening of an emergency session of the General Assembly. It should be noted that the General Secretary of the United Nations, in his statement of 27 March, alludes to the two principles of "respect for Iraq's sovereignty, territorial integrity and independence", on the one hand, and, on the other, "respect for the right of the Iraqi people to determine their future and to control their own natural resources." Europe's Council reacted, having its president say, "the unilateral use of force outside the international legal framework and without an explicit decision of the UN Security Council is in breach of international law. The UN Security Council needs our full support as the only authority to decide questions of peace and war". The Parliamentary Assembly of the Europe's Council decided to hold an urgent debate at its last ordinary session and adopted a resolution. The condemnation is quite explicit: "The Assembly recalls that since September 2002 it has taken a firm stand against the unilateral use of force outside the international legal framework and without explicit decision of the United Nations Security Council. In the absence of an explicit decision by the United Nations Security Council, it considers this attack unlawful and contrary to the principles of international law, which prohibits the use and threat of force except in cases provided for in the United States Charter. The Assembly is strongly concerned that intervention in Iraq, conducted in the name of preventive war, will compromise all the positive results achieved in safeguarding peace, collective security and international stability over the past fifty years and constitute a dangerous precedent of being exploited by other countries ". Eventually by the same countries, let's add! The Assembly also reiterated in the same resolution that the "belligerents" "may be brought to account for any crime against humanity or any war crime committed". On the other hand, the Ministers' Council of the Arabs States' League adopted a resolution on March 24 calling for "aggression against Iraq" and considered it "a violation of the UN Charter and the principles of international law" and "calls for the immediate and unconditional withdrawal of US-British invasion forces from Iraqi territory."

Let us add that since the outbreak of hostilities launched by the British-American coalition, a number of appeals have been made, including the International Commission of Jurists, the International Committee of the Red Cross and the Secretary-General of the United Nations, with a view to strict compliance with humanitarian law, including by the illegally attacked state, Iraq.. In conclusion, we should point out that the United Nations Commission on Human Rights rejected the German proposal, on behalf of the Western Group, to hold a special session on human rights and the humanitarian situation in Iraq as a result of the war.

III. The repression of international crimes

The repression of international crimes can take many forms, both nationally and internationally.

1. At the national level, the practice of the crime of aggression entails individual criminal responsibility and the international responsibility of States. International law still lacks many gaps in the forms that the legal responsibility of States may have. The responsibility is undoubtedly a political one, with the authorities that prepared and triggered the aggression to be dismissed or, at the very least, to suffer an electoral sanction. If that were the case, a process of impeachment would be underway in the United States, as the President supported hostilities in the war powers approved under the Constitution. In the presence of imperative international norms (jus cogens), the obligation of States to seek and punish perpetrators of international crimes can be defended; this is what the International Commission of Jurists recalled in a press release of 20 March last.

The principle of universal jurisdiction, which is compulsory for the States participating in the Geneva Convention, is not widely applied by the States, with Belgium at this level being the exception to the rule when this should be the principle. As regards war crimes, the four Geneva Conventions stipulate that any participating State, irrespective of the nationality of the alleged perpetrator of the acts or of the place where the offenses were committed, is under an obligation to repress the perpetrators of such acts. But political considerations, due to the repercussions on diplomatic relations, have often created obstacles to effective internal repression. If the Belgian judge can be legally held accountable, for example, by the families of the victims, by the crimes of the British-American forces, he alone will not be able to bring justice to the Iraqi people. Proof of this is the current situation: the

Belgian political authorities decided to transfer to the United States authorities on 20 May the war crimes complaint lodged on May 13 in Brussels by 17 Iraqis and two Jordanians against General Tommy Franks, commander of the US-British forces.

This possibility of transfer is allowed only recently and only after a change in the Belgian legislation on universal jurisdiction, which can happen when the complaints are considered "vexatious" and "unjustified". The Belgian authorities were especially sensitive to the US pressure to change NATO's facilities! On the other hand, there is a risk that the United States will institute a front-line justice with military tribunals that only condemn the crimes of the Iraqi authorities, even without respecting the fundamental rights of the accused and which are partial, which is contrary to their obligations to international right. There is always a suspicion of the risk of internal denial of justice for crimes involving high state authorities. Equally, it is not certain that the courts of the United Kingdom will judge those responsible for the crimes of this war; according to the Rome Statute establishing the International Criminal Court and of which the United Kingdom is a party, a case brought before the International Criminal Court cannot be accepted if it "is the subject of an investigation by a competent State to that end, unless that State is unwilling to conduct the investigation"(Article 17, 1, a).

2. In the face of this lack of national repression, we must turn to the international level.

Historically, in international law, in the face of conflicts involving several States, it is customary to set up international commissions of inquiry to gather information on the crimes committed and the responsibilities involved; This was the case in the two world conflicts of the twentieth century, as well as in the former Yugoslavia and

Rwanda; in the latter two were the conclusions of the committees which led to the creation of ad hoc international tribunals.

In addition to the desirable creation of such commission in the current situation, a court must judge the criminals. Nowadays, condemnation and repression are strongly opposed on the international scene, not the definition of aggression; proof of this is the non-inclusion of the crime of aggression in the drafting of the Rome Statute. According to Article 5 (2) of the Statute, "The Court shall exercise jurisdiction over the crime of aggression once a provision is adopted in accordance with articles 121 and 123 defining the crime and setting out the conditions under which the Court shall exercise jurisdiction with respect to this crime". So, the ICC is not currently competent to crack down on the crime of aggression, as some Western states, and particularly the United States, could not admit more than this because they are more often in the position of aggressor than of aggressor! Some southern States, notably most Arab States, refused to ratify the Statute, rightly claiming this gap regarding the crime of aggression.

The most plausible solution would be a temporary court. After the international tribunals for former Yugoslavia and Rwanda and the mixed courts for Cambodia and Sierra Leone, the time will come for a tribunal for Iraq. The responsibility of the governments for international crimes is a principle enshrined in international law. The trial is underway against Milosevic in the ICTY for the former Yugoslavia and the ICC for Rwanda condemned Jean Kambarda, Prime Minister of the Interim Government of Rwanda. The merits of international criminal law enforcement in relation to prosecution in national courts (despite the difficulties in the functioning of the courts for the former Yugoslavia and Rwanda, which have to be underlined, especially because of the insufficient cooperation of States, is a sine qua non on the proper administration of justice, whether it is the delivery and hearing of witnesses, the communication of evidence, etc.), have been underlined in doctrine. International tribunals are, in fact, better armed to convict crimes of this size.

In fact, its creation, because of the veto right of the United States and the United Kingdom cannot come from the Security Council. And then it could come from a resolution of the General Assembly to establish that court? This would not be the first time that the General Assembly would create a court.

The creation of a judicial body by another non-judicial body is allowed, considering that there is no delegation of the judicial function. The competence of the Security Council to create the ICC for the former Yugoslavia had been accepted as an instrument for the exercise of its principal function of maintaining peace and security.

The argument is transposable to the General Assembly due to the blocking of the Security Council, so the General Assembly replaces it in its peacekeeping function. The CFI for the former Yugoslavia, in the same mandate concerning the defense appeal invoking the preliminary objection of incompetence, even considered as an additional argument of legality the fact that its creation "has been approved and defended several times by the representative body of the United Nations, the General Assembly".

This would, in fact, give greater legitimacy to this court, the creation of which would be approved by the plenary body of the international community. The oppositions will undoubtedly be not of a legal nature, but of a political order.

This is because the crimes of the Anglo-American coalition are an attack on the fundamental interests of the international community and stir the conscience of all humanity (the mobilization of public opinion confirms it!), Which calls into question, is an absolute necessity the existence of the imperative rules of international law, the denunciation and repression of these odious crimes, so that the repetition of such acts tomorrow will be less tolerable and increasingly uncomfortable.

This "preventive" illegal war threatens the achievements of modern international law in the regulation of the law of war. But probably the most important is the clear disclosure of the gaps in the organization of today's international society, where values of justice and solidarity are missing.

It is time to rethink public international law to purge it of the flaws in the system that allow certain states to transform it into imperial law and so that international crimes committed by the most powerful states are not reduced to mere "collateral damage.".

The greatest threat to our societies is not insecurity (internally) or terrorism (at international level), as states have an interest in making people believe, it's injustice.

---

[1]. due to the alleged kidnapping and death by US intelligence agencies such as the NSA and CIA and the Dark Division 1 FOpEsp themselves, who have already demonstrated their efficiency and audacity in this regard.

[2]. troops formed by potential combat infantry military of 14 third world countries, under secret contract and under US command. Killer Shadow Troop or untrammeled troop, nicknames due to be the first to enter the battlefield without identification, without protection of land or air artillery, without being able to be disturbed by officers in the theater G, being oriented only by satellite communication.

[3]. here in particular, there were several deaths among the coalition soldiers who, unknowingly, used light ammunition containing or bathed in depleted uranium, practiced by military authorities and manufacturers of conventional weapons, which not only hit the enemy, its population as well as the invading troops.

CHAPTER 15

SOME THOUGHTS AND INFORMATION

When we think a little about Daniel's life and his stories, there are several aspects that draw our attention. Many of these issues have already been discussed for some time in the alternative media and some even in the traditional media.

Com a intenção de trazer um pouco mais de informação nesses tópicos, pesquisamos sobre algumas fontes curiosas de informação e resolvemos resumir os principais pontos neste capítulo, para servir de inspiração a você em pesquisas futuras e também de embasamento da história contada.

With the intention of bringing a little more information on these topics, we have researched some curious sources of information and decided to summarize the main points in this chapter, to inspire you in future research and also to support the story that we tell you here.

In addition, we also discussed these issues with our friend Rodrigo Romo – international speaker, creator and disseminator of the technique Rometria™, author of about 50 spiritual books with more than 70 thousand students around the world – and brought some interesting thoughts, thanks to its extensive knowledge about the subjects presented here, which we will present below.

ANTARCTICA

There is a lot of controversial information about the icy continent. Some of them official, others not so much. But there is no doubt that this piece of our planet generates curiosity and fascination. In Daniel's story, we have seen that he has visited the region a few times, and that he has had several encounters with nonhuman entities, including underground and secret training. This is only a fraction of what is told by several scholars mentioned or not in this book.

Antarctica is considered to be a continent that shelters diverse races – human and not human – that do not necessarily have a good relationship with each other.

The base – mentioned in the chapter in which Daniel visits the continent – belongs to what we call the fourth Reich – a continuation of the 3rd Nazi Reich of World War II, but with other goals and guidelines now. All this began when Adolf Hitler made a pact with reptilian beings in 1917, long before he took power. On that occasion, he received several maps of the region to explore its bases and later he would receive the contact of beings that we call "Nordic" – who founded with him the called fourth Reich.

This new organization is no longer concerned with Earth's problems, considering all the intergalactic knowledge it receives. Now they want the colonization of the solar system and, furthermore, genetic development through exchanges with this new "Norse" race – purer, in their view. We currently have about one million inhabitants at their bases on the icy continent and more than 40,000 people on bases around our solar system.

The greatest indicator of truthfulness from this information was the consequence of Operation HighJump – which was carried out by the US Navy between August 1946 and February 1947. The operation led by Richard Byrd Jr. (Rear Admiral) consisted of sending 4,700 men, 13 warships and about 33 aircraft with the official purpose of establishing a North American base in Antarctica called "Little America."

But let's face it ... Who carries such a heavy artillery to a continent of ice, only to establish a base? The official information is that the base was being built since August, and that by the end of February everyone had to return to the United States sooner as winter had arrived faster than normal. I was very surprised that the US Navy does not know the climate of the region and also does not know that the winter in the continent is in the middle of the year and not at the beginning of the year (because it is in the southern hemisphere).

Other relevant official information refers to "accidents" and their victims. Official losses of airplanes and ships in the region were reported due to the "weather conditions".

Now let's talk about unofficial information: the Americans went there to take the base from the 4th Reich, which was already established in the region a few years ago. As Nazi technology was far superior – even with an arsenal of extraterrestrial technology ships that had been made available to Germany years earlier – it was not difficult for them to defeat the navy in a short time, in the Antarctic summer, I might add.

Another interesting information is that the Fourth Reich is the only organization on Earth that has an agreement with the SGS here and the Aldebaran government. Therefore, the local Hidden Government would think twice before messing with them, as there is a stronger agreement with one of the factions of that system, which has a humanoid design.

The bases that exist in the icy continent are formed by large passages of dry volcanic lava of thousands of years ago, that formed great caves in the region. In them, ancient civilizations built their cities at a time when the axis of the Earth had a different angle and the south pole was closer to the Pacific Ocean.

Thus, with the pole shift and the end of ancient civilizations, these cities were covered with ice to be discovered and invaded by the Fourth Reich, shortly after its formation, when the Nazi party seized power in Germany in the 1930s.

The same was done by other extraterrestrial civilizations that have presence on the planet and, recently, by the hidden government that we will discuss soon after.

When I say "cities", I would like to make it clear that we are talking about places with streets, transports, buildings, houses and everything a "normal" city has. They are gigantic places that in some cases even have their own "sun" – an illumination technology that in addition to lightening the environment, still nourishes plants and animals as our sun does.

We can expect official information reporting ruins discovered in Antarctica soon in the traditional media. Unfortunately, some of this information serves as disinformation and distraction to the general population.

ALIENS

At least two extraterrestrial races were identified clearly in this book through Daniel's experiences. At the beginning of this book, with the only picture we have, we come across the being commonly known as "gray" – of short stature, big head and big eyes. The other being is the reptilian, with scaly skin, strong and with characteristic eyes of vertical pupils.

When Daniel met for the first time with the being that we called "gray" at the beginning of our history, we observe – also from the photos – the short stature, the gray color and the physical form that does not impose any fear. But in the course of the facts, we have seen that the little being manages to overcome and kill several men of the Special Force and the supporting army. Like Daniel, we also become thoughtful as we read, trying to figure out how this is possible.

In fact, the "gray" species is one of more than 380 ethnicities today in the universe. These species are derived from 78 descendant tribes of beings called Apician, a process that has occurred in the last five billion years of our timeline. Its original appearance varies from a few centimeters in height, up to about 1.80 m, and its skin ranges from darker shades, to shades of color closer to our skin – coppery – to slightly paler colorations.

The interesting thing was to discover in a conversation with Romo that these beings that Daniel found do not have gray skin. It is a uniform commonly used by members of the Intergalactic Federation – an association between beings from various systems that possess technology to travel between galaxies.

This uniform has technology that allows gravitational unfolding, working on the timeline, that is, it projects a type of force field that can be shaped according to demand. That is why the little being can move quickly and has tremendous strength. In fact, the impact is not on the being itself, but on the force field generated by his uniform. Another reason why the thousands of bullets fired by the command never hit the greys.

As a point of reference, science fiction has already illustrated this technology on some occasions. In the movie "Fantastic Four" (Marvel, 2015), this is precisely the technology used by the invisible woman. We can also see the same concept in the Star Trek Discovery (CBS, 2017) where the character Michael (Sonequa Martin-Green) at the end of the second season, wears a uniform that allows him to travel in time according to the gravitational manipulation of the line of time.

This uniform is made of an organic material and not synthetic, so it looks like these beings are naked. It's like a second, living skin, being part of your body – giving command for neural control.

Grays are basically beings that work for some reptilian ethnicities. The Royal White Draco, for example – even mentioned several times by Corey Goode in their stories – uses these beings as their front line, exactly as shown in the movie "Jupiter Ascending" (Warner, 2015). Once again, fiction imitates reality.

FIGURE 19. Representation of the Royal White Draco by the story of Corey Goode. Credits: TV Gaia.

But the most common function is to collect organic material. In Daniel's story, we saw that the little beings took all the blood from the captured bodies before removing them, we can even see spots in the photo. This is another classic characteristic of them: for both humans and animals, they paralyze and bleed out their victims before transport.

The bodies captured are used to create clones that feed reptilians; also, for genetic research to understand some species developments; to decipher some "missing links"; or for hormonal extraction for synthesis purposes. Some hormones serve as "recreational drugs" to some species. Corey Goode has also mentioned all this in his reports, including cases of "genetic piracy", where human members of the Hidden Government traffic human material in exchange for technology and favors.

The reptilian being, described later in the chapter "Unusual encounter in Colombia", comes from draconian intraterrestrial beings derived from the entities we call Archons. To understand this, I need to tell a story.

The beings commonly called Annunaki are entities that came from the constellation of Pleiades to Earth about 450,000 years ago. When they arrived here, they found some humanoids inhabiting the planet peacefully alongside Agarthians, beings that come from the reptilians – inhabiting both the surface and the intrasphere.

The Annunaki came to Earth primarily attracted by the extraction of some special minerals and to research in this mineral field. Thus, they installed several mining and metal processing plants around the globe. One of these mills was dangerously close to two Agarthian cities: Sodom and Gomorrah.

Feeling threatened, the reptilians invaded the Annunaki ore processing station and destroyed it. As a retaliation, the Annunaki detonated three nuclear warheads in the Agartian cities, killing close to eleven million beings, beginning a war between humanoids and reptilians on Earth.

These draconian intraterrestrial beings, whom Daniel encountered on his mission, are remnants of this war and are part of a rebellious faction that still lives here. It is not very clear in what dimension they live, since they pass between the fourth and the fifth.

They are rebellious, do not follow a clear command line and do not have an established goal. They had been asleep for about twenty thousand years but were awakened by some projects such as Montauk and Philadelphia, both American government, which are intended to carry out time and interdimensional journeys.

When awakened, they attempted an association with the US government, but without success. Then they became partners of the former Nazi Germany, through the exchange of technology, supplies and knowledge. Nowadays there is no way to know their intentions and their goals here on Earth are not clear, only the remaining anger they have for humans because of the Annunaki conflict.

EXTRACTION OF ARTIFACTS

We saw in Daniel's story that many of his missions were related to the extraction of ancient artifacts, with supposedly extraterrestrial technology, especially in the Middle East region.

As published in the June 2014 Science magazine, Earth has "a vast reservoir of water sufficient to fill the Earth's oceans three times" below the surface in the earth's crust. In the last passage of the planet Nibiru by the solar system, about 12,000 years ago, the gravitational force changed the Earth's axis by approximately 40 degrees of inclination. The consequence of this was the change of the magnetic and physical poles, breaking the crust in some points and releasing part of this underground water to the oceans on the surface.

This generated the famous "flood," which we already know through the Christian Bible, which flooded thousands of cities and bases across the globe, forcing its inhabitants to abandon them as quickly as possible.

Another effect of the passage of Nibiru on Earth was an electromagnetic discharge between the two planets and Mars, which caused ships that were close to our planet to fall and those that were lodged here could not get out.

FIGURE 20: Stargate from the Stargate SG-1 series. Credit: Internet.

All these factors added to the electromagnetic pulse and the wreckage of the war between the Annunaki and the Agartians, form these artifacts that are being recovered with the help of Daniel and his former team. All this technology and information that is under debris is being revealed. In this sense, the Middle East region is a very rich territory, because there were the main bases of Annunaki and Agarthian.

There is much more to be discovered, and the general public does not know anything. In the Sudan region there is a vast array of artifacts that cannot be carved out by political problems. Another very rich region is the Amazon. Numerous pyramids, ships and cities are hidden beneath the dense rainforest.

The most coveted artifact is the so-called "Stargate," so well portrayed in the Stargate SG-1 series (MGM, 1997-2007) used for travel through "wormholes" – interdimensional passages – that go from one place to another of the galaxy instantly.

If you think this is just science fiction, think again: Dr. Michael Salla, one of the world's leading exopolitics authorities, recently presented a thanksgiving scene for the Stargate Atlantis series (2004-2009), derived from the aforementioned SG-1. There is a thank you to the "American space force". Recalling that ten years ago President Trump hadn't been elected and much less signed the creation of that same American military division.

WHO'S IN CHARGE?

One of the most frequently asked questions about the history of this book is: Who commands this world elite? I cannot think of a better answer than a hidden government.

The domination and manipulation made by few families and secret orders throughout the history of humankind is widely studied and known by many people. It was only recently formed, we would say between the First and Second World War, a hidden and organized government on our planet.

Today it has its claws nailed to practically every nation on the globe and governs all countries through the socio-cultural-political illusion. This hidden government pitted against each other using the logic "divide to conquer". And just watch the useless fight between right and left in virtually every election on Earth.

But the answer may not be that simple.

The idea of having an elite troop interfering in some earthly affairs came from the so-called Galactic Alliance. It is not necessarily a part of the group we call the Hidden Government, but it has interests in human development and in how things are conducted here.

The problem lies in the political relationship of this alliance with the Hidden Government. That is why we see a contradictory behavior in the missions Daniel participates. Protecting and then attacking the same side. One hour covering non-human entities and at other times directly interfering with their interests.

This alliance is the set of interplanetary federations. Part of this group has political dissent with other groups present here on the planet. Notice that the phrase "up there, like down here" has never been so true.

While the alliance was interested in helping or "cutting the wings" of groups according to their interests, the Secret Land Government that effectively operated the elite troop harvested information and technology from the missions for their personal use here on the planet. The SGS, as this government is called, played a double game with the different races of aliens and with the federations, hanging where it interested them more.

The Alliance, on the other hand, makes deals with the main SGS countries on Earth without really knowing that all of this is happening. Thus, the command of the alliance through the Secret Government of the Earth ends up being ambiguous and serving political purposes according to the interests of the moment.

CHAPTER **16**

THE FINAL JUDGMENT

Throughout the period that Daniel was transported from prisons and barracks by different countries, no one ever warned him or talked to him about what was happening; until the last moment.

In the chapter "Back Home," Daniel is released from the barracks in Rio Grande, goes to Porto Alegre and finally goes by bus to Brasilia, where his family lived. But that's not the whole story.

Now, let's get to know the story of his judgment, which would change his life forever.

On his last day in jail at Rio Grande barracks, Daniel slept in his cell when he was caught in the middle of the night by one of the soldiers, who asked him to pack his things. The order was to be ready in thirty minutes, which he fulfilled, as always.

While leaving the cell, the soldiers placed a blindfold on him. What he was able to realize was that minutes later he got into a car and was taken to an airport after a journey of about an hour. From there, still blindfolded, he boarded a plane where he stayed for about an hour or two. When getting off the aircraft, still blindfolded, he was put back in a car where he stayed for another thirty minutes until finally arriving at the destination and having his sales withdrawn.

Daniel did not know where he was, or whether he was still in Brazil or in a neighboring country. What he could see was a kind of garage in the basement with a door in the background and nothing else. Beside him, four soldiers in different uniforms escorted him.

As he passed the door, he saw that the place was actually a prison, for there were four empty cells. Then he was placed in one of them, where he would stay for the next three days.

The cell was reasonably comfortable. It had about 5 mx 5 m, two bunk beds, a private bathroom with hot water, a small table with water, biscuits and some newspapers for reading – in Portuguese, this time. As there were no windows in the cell, it was impossible to know if it was still night or if it was already daylight. But because he was tired, he decided to get some sleep.

His routine on these three days was basically the same: he had six meals a day and exercised inside the cell because he was not allowed to leave at any time. The most curious fact of this stay was that Daniel was visited by five generals and seven colonels while he was there. Everyone, without exception, asked about their previous work and wanted to know details of how it was and the most interesting information. Our fighter did not reveal any information since he was still under oath.

His last day of jail was a Wednesday. On that day, a guy who was different from the army officers came to visit him. He was a thin, tall, bearded civilian who talked to him about math, calculations, and so on. In the end, he left one of these crossword journals as a gift. To this day Daniel does not know the reason or who could be this guy.

Soon after, a soldier came to give some orders and messages to Daniel. The officer brought him a full uniform and asked him to put on his uniform and get ready to leave. Then a young man came to cut his hair (shaved) and his beard to give him the usual military look.

His uniform was very interesting. Of dark gray color, it contained the badges referring to his patent (at that moment of 2nd Sergeant) and also the flag with the universal symbol. It was rectangular with the drawing of the continents in the middle. Above, an old-style sword – like those of the Templars – with its spear turned to the left and down another equal sword, but with the spear to the right. In the two corners of the upper rectangle, there was a drawing of an oval disk (like a classic UFO) and right in the center of the continents map was a silhouette of a skeleton's skull.

Still speaking of his uniform, he could see all the symbols of all his acquired specialties while serving the elite world troupe, such as chemist, jungle, parachuting, and so on. Everything he knew and did was represented in that official uniform.

After shaving his head, he showered and put on his uniform. A few hours passed and nothing happened. Daniel called the soldier guarding the cell and asked him what time it would be. The anxiety of knowing what was happening was consuming him. He did not know if he would be freed, transferred, or anything else, but surely it was all right for him to wear that uniform at that moment. How many memories!

It was then that, shortly after his last meal that it was a dinner around midnight, an illustrious figure came to his cell. He was a minister of the Brazilian government. His Excellency greeted him, holding both his hands and said looking into his eyes, "I have much respect and gratitude for your services." Daniel, who was thrilled, thanked him.

The minister went on to explain that he would be his defense representative. With two matching envelopes in his hands, he placed them before Daniel and explained that he would have five minutes to make a choice.

The envelope on the left would lead him to sign an agreement in which he would be held for thirty-five years in the Guantanamo military prison, located in Cuba and managed by the United States. In that case, he would have the salary maintained for the whole time in 30% of his earnings, which would be received by a relative of his nomination. In addition, Daniel would maintain his position, courses and patent, and could eventually return to activity after imprisonment, obviously depending on his age and ability to contribute. But he would have to spend every minute of the thirty-five years to which he was sentenced in prison.

The envelope on the right contained an agreement that Daniel would be "deleted." This meant that he would be free and could walk away immediately, but that everything, without exception, from a few years before his entry into the Brazilian army until that moment would be erased from world history. All courses, jobs, monetary transactions ... Everything! The only requirement would be for him to forget everything he did and say no more about it, with the death penalty – without warning – if he failed to reach agreement.

The minister said he would be back in five minutes and the decision should already be made. So he turned and left. Just in time, six soldiers and a sergeant arrived in his cell. The sergeant asked for the envelope and Daniel handed the chosen one over.

The soldiers and the sergeant then escorted him to a room by the cell where there was a booth. They handed over all the necessary paperwork and waited, for about ten minutes, for their release. So a door opened and they passed into a room about fifty feet away where there was an elevator. They all went in, and the last floor, the sixth, was pressed. Daniel then finally learned that he was being held in the basement of a building, somewhere unknown.

When the doors opened, the minister waited for him. From there they followed them and the officers to a door which, when opened, revealed a siding – which was probably there to prevent even when the door opened, someone could see what was going on inside.

When the doors opened, the minister waited for him. From there, the entire group went to a door that, when opened, revealed a siding – which was probably there to avoid that even when the door opened, someone could see what was going on inside.

The two then skirted the obstacle and came upon a room that looked like a courtroom. Four officers sat at the front and two chairs were placed in the middle: one for Daniel and one for the minister. Behind, some soldiers guarded and secured the place.

Immediately as they sat down, they gave a headset and asked Daniel to put it on. He obeyed. Thus, they began to read a document in English, then in Russian, in Chinese, and finally in Portuguese. It was the same document that described Daniel's entire trajectory, from his enlistment to that very moment, the accusations made, and the reason he was there at that moment. The headset was a simultaneous translation.

At the end of the reading, Daniel was already treated as a convict. Since he had chosen the envelope on the right, he began the process of "delete". At that very moment, one of the members of the table declared that he could not leave the room with the uniform he had on his body. He asked the "convict" to approach the table for the final reading.

While the subject read all the courses, achievements, and missions in which Daniel had participated, a soldier was removing his patents, courses and banners from his uniform and placing the objects on a tray next to him. Upon finishing the accessories, the officer took off his uniform: his shoes, socks, pants and shirt, leaving Daniel only in his underwear in court.

That was the first moment Daniel really felt on the skin what it would be like to lose everything, literally. He did not think it was like that. Behind him, he recognized an American major, who closed the ceremony and asked the soldiers to escort Daniel back to the cell.

When he reached the cell accompanied by the minister, he noticed that he let a few tears escape. He told Daniel that the situation was unfortunate and wished him good luck. "Now everything is going to change," he murmured as he wiped his face.

As our combatant had no clothes to wear, the minister had them bring a set that Daniel could wear. Before leaving, the Excellency still lent him some money so that he could secure his return home.

It was then that three soldiers arrived and said it was time for Daniel to leave. At that moment, he was again blindfolded and put in a vehicle, which headed to the airport again. After some time of flight, landed and again our combatant was placed in a car that left him at the bus station in Porto Alegre, Rio Grande do Sul.

Daniel, not knowing what to do or what to think, sat on the floor and meditated for a moment. A movie passed before his eyes. Everything that happened, from his leaving the Brazilian army until that moment, his last mission, all the prisons around the world until arriving at his judgment and the decision that he had to do.

He also thought of all the technologies he had access to during his time in the elite world troupe. Things that the general public never imagined at the time, such as training with holograms and laser weapons. And what about the clashes with nonhuman beings?

Then Daniel took a bus to Brasilia. A few hours later, as we told earlier, he was received by his parents at home. For the next three years, he would still believe that all this was a misunderstanding. That in fact, at some point, he would be forgiven and would be able to return to the troop. He never imagined that "deleting" was like this. He had no more bank account, he had nothing else. When looking for a job, not even high school was in his history.

And now, what to do?

Made in the USA
Las Vegas, NV
14 August 2023